P9-EME-074

# *New Testament* BIBLE STORY BOOK

by Daniel Partner

Illustrated by Kathy Arbuckle

© MCMXCVI by Barbour & Company, Inc.

ISBN 1-55748-926-2

All rights reserved. No part of this publication may be reproduced or transmitted in any form or by any means without written permission of the publisher.

EXCLUSIVE DISTRIBUTION BY PARADISE PRESS

Printed in the United States of America

**30656**

# *New Testament*
# BIBLE STORY BOOK

# Zechariah Sees An Angel
### Luke 1:1-23

Just before Jesus Christ was born, king Herod ruled Judea for the Roman Empire. Herod had rebuilt the ancient Jewish temple. There a priest helped with the worship. His name was Zechariah; his wife was Elizabeth.

One day, Zechariah was ministering in the Holy Place. Outside the court was full of worshipers. Suddenly, he saw an angel. Zechariah was terrified.

"Fear not," the angel said. "God has heard your prayer. Elizabeth will have a baby boy. You'll name him John. Many will rejoice when he's born. He'll have Elijah's spirit and turn many to the Lord."

"How will I know this is true?" questioned Zechariah. "I'm an old man and my wife is old too."

"I'm Gabriel," said the angel. "God sent me to give you good news. But you don't believe me. I said that this will happen, but you won't speak until it does."

When Zechariah came out the people could tell he'd seen a vision. He tried to signal to them but they couldn't understand. When his service in the temple was over, Zechariah went home.

*Questions: What did the angel tell Zechariah? Why couldn't Zechariah speak after he saw the angel?*

## Gabriel Greets Mary
### *Luke 1:26-38*

"This is what God has done for me!" praised Elizabeth. She had just learned she and Zechariah were to have a baby.

Next God sent the angel Gabriel to Nazareth. This town is in Galilee north of Judea. Living there was a girl named Mary who was to wed Joseph.

"Greetings," Gabriel said. "You are God's favorite woman. God is with you.

"What kind of speaking is this?" Mary wondered.

"Don't be afraid," Gabriel continued. "You're going to have a baby boy. You'll call his name Jesus. He'll be called the Son of God."

*Questions: What did Elizabeth do when she knew she would have a baby? What did Gabriel tell Mary?*

# The Birth of John the Baptist
### Luke 1:39-80

"Hello, Elizabeth." Mary had come to see her cousin Elizabeth. When Elizabeth heard Mary's voice, her baby jumped inside her. She was filled with the Holy Spirit.

"Mary! You are the most blessed of all women," Elizabeth exclaimed. "Your baby is blessed too. Why has my Lord's mother come to see me? When I heard your voice, my baby jumped for joy in me."

Some months later Elizabeth's baby, John, was born. He would grow up in the wilderness— a Nazarite priest for God. This was the last prophet—John the Baptist.

*Questions: What happened when Elizabeth heard Mary's voice? Who was Elizabeth's son?*

7

# The Birth of Jesus Christ
## Matthew 1:18-21; Luke 2:1-7

Joseph was a carpenter in Nazareth. He was soon to be Mary's husband. One night he had a dream. In it an angel spoke: "Joseph take Mary as your wife. The child in her is from the Holy Spirit. When he's born, call him Jesus. He'll save his people from their sins."

In those days Emperor Augustus Caesar commanded that his people be counted. To do this everyone went to their hometown. For Mary and Joseph this was Bethlehem. Bethlehem was also King David's hometown.

It was a long journey from Nazareth to Bethlehem. Mary, who was almost ready to have her baby, traveled with Joseph. They went down the hills in Galilee to the Jordan River. Then they followed the river to Judea. Up in the Judean hills they came to Bethlehem. The town was full of people who had come to be counted. An inn was there, but it was full of people.

Suddenly, Mary had to give birth. So they went into a stable. Here Mary had her child, Jesus. She wrapped him in a blanket and put him to sleep in a feed trough.

*Questions: What did the angel tell Joseph that Jesus would do? Where was Jesus born?*

# The Angel's Announcement
### Luke 2:8-20

That night, shepherds guarded their sheep near Bethlehem. Suddenly, they were surrounded with light. An angel stood there. The shepherds were terrified.

"Don't be afraid. I've come to give you good news. Today, in Bethlehem, Christ the Lord has been born. You'll find him wrapped in a blanket; sleeping in a feed trough."

Suddenly, the sky was filled with angels praising God. "Glory to God in heaven. On earth, peace and good will."

"Let's go to Bethlehem and see this wonderful thing."

And they did. There they found Mary, Joseph, and Jesus, as the angels said.

*Questions: Who did the angels say was born? What did the angels say when they praised God?*

9

# The Praise of Simeon
### Luke 2:21-35

An old man named Simeon stood in the temple at Jerusalem. In his arms was the baby Jesus. Simeon praised God:

Thank you Lord for letting me leave this life
   in peace.
I've finally seen your salvation for all people.
He's a light so the Gentiles can see you;
And he's the glory of your people Israel.

Mary and Joseph had brought Jesus to the temple. The law said they should promise him to God. The Spirit told Simeon to be there too.

"Many in Israel will rise and fall because of Him," Simeon told Jesus's parents.

*Questions: What did Simeon say about Jesus? Why did Mary and Joseph bring Jesus to the Temple?*

# The Rising Star of Christ
## Matthew 2:1-10

In the East, far from Bethlehem lived some very wise men who studied the stars. They traveled to Jerusalem to ask one question: "Where is the child who's born to be king of the Jews? We saw his star rise in the sky. So we came to honor him."

When King Herod heard this he was afraid he would lose his kingdom. "Call the chief priests and scribes," he ordered. "They'll know where the Christ is to be born."

The Jewish priests explained to Herod the prophet Micah's words:

Bethlehem in Judea is one of your
littlest towns.
But out of her will come the ruler of Israel.

Secretly Herod spoke to the wise men from the East: "When you've found the child, tell me. I want to honor him too."

When they had heard the king, the men set out. There, ahead of them, went the star they had seen rising. It stopped over a house in Bethlehem. The travelers were overcome by joy.

*Questions: What were the men from the East looking for? How did the priests know where Jesus would be born?*

# Precious Gifts for Jesus
### Matthew 2:11-14

The joyous men entered the house and saw the child with Mary. They knelt down with reverence. Then, opening their treasure chests, they offered Jesus gifts. They gave him precious gold, frankincense, and myrrh.

When the men left, they didn't return to Herod. In a dream, one of them had been warned not to do this. So they traveled back to their land by another road.

Joseph saw an angel in a dream. "Hurry away to Egypt," the angel said. "Herod wants to kill the child."

That night the family left for Egypt.

*Questions: What gifts did the men give Jesus? Why didn't they go back to Herod?*

# Christ is Hidden in Egypt
## Matthew 2:15-23

Herod was angry when he saw he'd been tricked by the wise men. He ordered his solders to kill all the babies in Bethlehem. He wanted to be sure he killed the king of the Jews.

Hundreds of years before, Jeremiah said this would happen:

I hear a voice in Ramah, near Bethlehem.
It is Rachel crying for her children.
She won't be comforted
because they are gone.

But Jesus was safe with his family in Egypt.

When Herod died an angel came to Joseph in a dream. "Get up and go back to Israel," the angel said. "Those who want to kill the child are dead." Long before, a prophet had spoken of this: "Out of Egypt I've called my son," he wrote.

But the family didn't return to Judea. Herod's son was ruling there and Joseph was afraid. Again, he'd been warned in a dream. So Joseph took Mary and Jesus to Nazareth in Galilee. There they were safe. Another old prophet had seen this would happen. He said, "He will be called a Nazarene."

*Questions: Why did Herod kill the children of Bethlehem? Why did Joseph go to live in Nazareth?*

13

# In His Father's House
### Luke 2:40-52

Jesus grew and became strong. He was full of wisdom and God preferred him.

When Jesus was twelve years old, his family went to Jerusalem for the Passover. Afterwards, they started home, but the boy Jesus stayed behind in Jerusalem. When they couldn't find him they returned to Jerusalem. There they searched for Jesus.

After three days they found him in the temple. The teachers were amazed at his understanding and answers. When his parents saw him they were surprised. His mother said, "Child, why have you treated us like this? Your father and I have been looking for you. We've been worried sick".

"Why were you searching for me?" Jesus asked her. "Didn't you know that I would be in my Father's house?" But they didn't understand his meaning.

Then Jesus went down with them from Jerusalem. They retuned to Nazareth and he obeyed them. His mother always remembered the things he did and said.

Jesus grew in wisdom and in years. He was preferred by God and the people.

*Questions: Why did Jesus and his family go to Jerusalem? What was Jesus doing when they found him?*

# The Work of John the Baptist
### Luke 3:1-14

John, the son of Elizabeth and Zechariah, lived in the wilderness. Zechariah's son was also Israel's last prophet. When he was thirty, God sent him to the Jewish people. He told them to turn from sin and be forgiven. John baptized those who turned from sin in the Jordan River.

Earlier the prophet Isaiah spoke of John the Baptist:

> His voice is crying in the wilderness.
> He will go ahead of the Lord to
>     make the paths straight for him.
> Then everyone will see God's salvation.

John the Baptist wore rough clothes woven from camel's hair and a leather belt. He ate dried grasshoppers and wild honey from the trees. John's words were different too. He said: "Turn from sin and do right. The kingdom of heaven is nearby. Its king will soon be here."

Pharisees were men of Israel who made a show of being good. John told them, "You're the children of snakes. Who told you to escape from God's anger against you?"

*Questions: What did John the Baptist tell the people? What did he do when they turned from sin?*

# John Baptizes Jesus
### Luke 3:12-22; Matthew 3:13-17

"I wonder if he's Christ?" Everyone wondered about John the Baptist.

"I baptize you with water," he answered. "The one who's coming is greater than I am. He'll baptize you with the Holy Spirit and fire." John was speaking of Jesus.

Jesus came to be baptized by John. But John said, "You should baptize me."

"It's proper for us to do this," Jesus answered. "We'll be doing what's right."

John baptized Jesus. Just then God's Spirit came down like a dove. And God spoke: "This is my Son whom I love. He pleases me."

*Questions: What happened when Jesus was baptized? What did God say about Jesus?*

16

# The Devil Tempts Jesus
## Luke 4:1-11

The Spirit of God led Jesus into the wilderness. There he was tempted by the devil. When he was hungry, the devil came. "If you're God's Son, make these stones into bread."

"One doesn't only live on bread. God's words are food as well."

The devil took him to the temple roof. "The angels won't let you get hurt," he tempted. "So jump to the ground."

"It's written, 'Don't put God to the test.'"

"I'll give you all of earth's kingdoms; worship me!" commanded Satan.

"Get away Satan! The Bible says, 'Worship and serve only God.'"

*Questions: Bread is food. What else did Jesus say is food? What does the Bible say about worship?*

17

# Jesus Finds His Followers
*John 1:29-41*

When the devil left Jesus alone, angels came and cared for him. Then he went back to where John was by the Jordan River. John saw Jesus coming toward him. "Look! It's the Lamb of God who takes away the world's sin. This is the one I said was greater than I am. I've seen this, and now I tell you: This is the Son of God!"

The next morning John was standing with two of his followers. Jesus walked by. John shouted, "Look, here is the Lamb of God!" His two followers heard this and followed Jesus.

Jesus turned around and said, "What are you looking for?"

"Teacher," they replied, "where do you live?"

"Come and see."

One man, Andrew, found his brother Simon and said, "We've found the Christ!" He brought Simon to Jesus.

Jesus looked at Simon and said, "You are John's son Simon. But your new name is Peter."

The next day Jesus went to Galilee. He said to Philip "Follow me."

Later Jesus met Nathaniel who said: "Teacher, you're the Son of God! You're the King of Israel!"

*Questions: What did John the Baptist say Jesus was? Who did Nathaniel say Jesus was?*

18

# "You'll fish for people"
### Matthew 4:18-22

Jesus walked by the Sea of Galilee. There he saw Peter and Andrew again. They were casting a net into the sea because they were fishermen. He said to them, "Follow me and you'll fish for people."

Right away they left their nets and followed him. Farther down the beach Jesus saw two other brothers. James and John were in a fishing boat with their father Zebedee. They were mending their nets. Jesus called to them. At once, they left their father in the boat and followed him.

*Questions: What were Peter and Andrew doing when Jesus called them? What were James and John doing when Jesus called them?*

# The Miracle at the Wedding
*John 2:1-11*

Jesus and his followers went to a town called Cana. There was a wedding in that town. Everyone was having fun and eating a big meal. But before the meal was over, they ran out of wine. Mary, Jesus' mother, knew he could help. Mary said to Jesus, "They have no wine." He said, "It is not time for me to do miracles." But Mary told the people, "Do what he tells you to do."

Six big stone jars were standing there. They each held as much water as a bathtub. Jesus said, "Fill those jars with water." The servants did what he said. Then Jesus told them, "Take some of it to the leader of this wedding." So they dipped some water out of the jars. It had changed to wine.

The leader of the wedding was surprised. He spoke to the bridegroom. "This wine is better than any you have served so far. You kept the best wine until last."

This was the first time Jesus did something to prove he was the Son of God. When his followers saw it, they believed in Jesus even more.

*Questions: What happened to the water? Why did Jesus change the water into wine?*

# Cleansing His Father's House
## John 2:13-22

Jesus went up to Jerusalem for the Passover. In the temple he found people selling sheep and doves for sacrifices. There were money changers at their tables. Jesus made a whip out of cords. He used it to drive these people out of the temple. He chased their sheep into the street and poured out their coins.

"Take these things out of here," he shouted. "Stop making my Father's house a marketplace!"

The Jews said to him, "What right do you have to do this? Show us a sign that God's given you control of the temple."

"Here's your sign," Jesus said: "Destroy this temple and in three days I'll raise it up."

"It's taken forty-six years to build this temple. Its not finished yet," the Jews said. "Will you raise it up in three days?"

But Jesus wasn't talking about that temple on Mount Moriah. He was speaking of the temple of his body. They would put him to death. But he would come back from death in three days. His followers remembered that he'd said this. So when Jesus returned from death they believed his words.

*Questions: What did Jesus use to drive the people out of the temple? What did Jesus mean when he said he'd raise up the temple in three days?*

21

# "I'll be lifted up on a cross"
## John 3:1-21

Nicodemus visited Jesus at night. He was a Pharisee and a leader of the Jews. "We know you're a teacher from God," he said. "No one can do these things unless God is with him."

"I'll tell you the truth," Jesus answered. "No one can see God's kingdom without being born of the Spirit."

"How can an old man be born again?"

Whatever is born of a woman is human. Whatever is born of the Spirit is spirit."

"How can this be?" Nicodemus wondered.

"Are you a teacher of Israel?" Jesus asked. "Yet you don't understand?" Then Jesus said: "Remember how Moses lifted up a brass serpent on a pole? Whoever saw it was healed of the snakes' poison."

"Yes," said Nicodemus.

"Well, I'm the Son of Man. I'll be lifted up on a cross. Whoever believes in me will be healed of sin and have eternal life. Because God loved the world so much that he gave his only Son. Whoever believes in him won't die forever. They'll have eternal life."

*Questions: How can a person see God's kingdom? What happens when a person believes in Jesus?*

# The Woman at Jacob's Well
## Part One
### John 4:7-18

Jesus traveled from Judea to Samaria. About noontime, Jesus rested by Jacob's well, and His followers went to buy food.

A woman came to the well to draw water. "Give me a drink," Jesus said.

"You're a Jew," she said. "I'm a Samaritan. Jews don't share with Samaritans."

"You don't know who's asking you for a drink. If you did, you'd ask me for a drink. Then I'd give you living water."

"You don't have a bucket, sir. How will you get that living water?"

"Whoever drinks water from this well," Jesus said, "will get thirsty again. But when I give you water the well is inside of you. It bubbles up to give you eternal life."

"Sir," the woman said, "please give me this water. Then I'll never thirst again. I won't have to come to this well."

"Go get your husband, and come back."

"I don't have a husband."

"What you say is true," Jesus said. "You've had five husbands. And the man you have now isn't your husband."

*Questions: What kind of water does Jesus give? What does this water give you?*

23

# The Woman at Jacob's Well
## Part Two
### John 4:19-42

The Samaritan woman said, "I see you're a prophet. Tell me, which is right, to worship at this mountain or at Jerusalem?"

"Believe me," Jesus answered. "The time has come when you won't worship the Father in either place. The real worshipers worship the Father in spirit and in truth. God is seeking people who will worship him this way. You see, God is Spirit. So the people who worship him must worship in spirit and truth."

Then the woman said, "I know Christ is coming. When he does he'll teach us everything."

"I'm speaking to you. I'm Christ."

Just then Jesus' followers came back with the food. They were surprised that Jesus was talking with this Samaritan woman. She left her water jug at the well and hurried back to town. "Come and see a man who told me everything I've ever done! Could he be Christ?"

Many people in that town believed in Jesus because of the woman. Jesus stayed there two days. Many more believed because they heard his words.

*Questions: How did Jesus say people should worship the Father? What happened to the people in the town because of the woman at the well?*

# A Nobleman's Household Believes
### John 4:46-5:1

When Jesus got back to Galilee the people welcomed him. They had seen what he'd done in Jerusalem. Jesus went to Cana where he changed the water into wine. In nearby Capernaum there was a nobleman whose son was sick. He heard that Jesus had come from Judea. This man went up the hills from the seashore to see Jesus. He begged him: "Come and heal my son. He's about to die."

"Unless you see miracles you won't believe," Jesus replied.

The nobleman said, "Sir, come down before by little boy dies."

"Go, your son will live."

The man believed Jesus' words and started for home. On the way the next day his slaves met him. "Your child is alive!" they exclaimed.

He asked them what time the boy began to get well. "Yesterday at one in the afternoon his fever went down." That was the exact hour that Jesus said, "Your son will live." So the nobleman believed as did all his household.

This was the second time Jesus did something to prove he was the Son of God.

*Questions: When Jesus said his son would live, what did the nobleman do? Who else believed when the nobleman believed?*

# Trouble in Nazareth
### Part One
### Luke 4:16-24

Jesus went back to His hometown of Nazareth. In the Synagogue, Jesus stood up to read from the sixty-first chapter of Isaiah.

The Spirit of the Lord is upon me. I'm anointed to bring good news to the poor. He has sent me to call out "freedom!" to the captives and give sight to the blind; to let the overloaded people go free; and to proclaim the year of God's grace to everyone.

Then Jesus rolled up the scroll and handed it back. Everyone was looking at him. He said, "Today these words have come true." Everyone was amazed at his gracious words.

But then someone said, "Isn't this Joseph's son? We know his brothers and sisters. How can he teach us?"

Jesus said, "You're thinking: 'Why doesn't he do miracles like he did in Capernaum?' I'll tell you the truth. A prophet is never welcome in his hometown."

*Questions: What is one thing the Scripture said Jesus had come to do? Why did the people question Jesus?*

# Trouble in Nazareth
*Part Two*
*Luke 4:24-32*

"I'll tell you the truth. A prophet is never welcome in his own hometown." Jesus was speaking with the people in the synagogue in Nazareth.

"In Elijah's time it didn't rain for three and a half years. There were many widows in Israel. But which widow did God tell Elijah to help? A woman who was outside of Israel; not a Jew. And weren't there many lepers in Israel in Elisha's time? But the only leper the prophet healed was Naaman from Syria."

When they heard this everyone in the synagogue was enraged. They wanted miracles like in Capernaum. They got up and drove Jesus out of town. Nazareth was built on a hillside. They led him up to the top of the highest hill. They wanted to throw him off the cliff. But Jesus slipped away from them and went on his way. It wasn't yet time for him to die.

In Capernaum by the Sea of Galilee, Jesus taught the next sabbath day. They were amazed at his teaching. Unlike other teachers, Jesus spoke like an expert.

*Questions: What example did Jesus give that shows a prophet isn't welcome in his hometown? Why were the people angry at Jesus?*

27

# "You're the Son of God!"
## Luke 4:33-41

In Capernaum lived a man who was controlled by a demon. He saw Jesus and the demon cried out: "Let us alone, Jesus of Nazareth! Have you come to destroy us? I know you, you're the Holy One of God."

Jesus commanded the demon, "Be silent and come out of him!" The demon threw the man down on the ground and came out. The man wasn't hurt.

Everyone around was amazed. "What kind of speaking is this?" they wondered. "He has power to command the evil spirits. And out they come!" The reports about Jesus were heard everywhere.

After this Jesus entered Peter's house. There, Peter's mother-in-law was suffering with a high fever. They asked him about her. Jesus stood over the woman and rebuked the fever. It left her. Right away Peter's mother-in-law got out of bed. She served them their meal.

As the sun was setting, people brought the sick to Jesus. He put his hands on them and cured them. Demons came out of many people, shouting, "You're the Son of God!" Jesus wouldn't let the demons speak because they knew he was Christ.

*Questions: What did Jesus do to make the demons leave? Why wouldn't Jesus let the demons speak?*

# "Let down your nets for fish."
## Luke 5:1-11

Once Jesus was beside the Sea of Galilee. Nearby were two fishing boats, belonging to Peter and Andrew and James and John. These young disciples were nearby washing their nets. Jesus stepped into Peter's boat and sat teaching the crowds.

Jesus finished teaching. "Peter," he said, "put out into deep water and let down your nets for fish."

"Master," Peter answered, "we've worked all night long and caught nothing. But if you say so, I'll let down the nets." When they did, they caught so many fish their nets were breaking. Peter signaled James and John who came and filled both boats to overflowing!

Overwhelmed with God's wonder, he fell down and cried, "Go away from me, Lord. I'm a sinful man!"

"Don't be afraid," Jesus comforted Peter. "From now on you'll catch people." The young men left their boats and all they had and followed Jesus.

*Questions: Why did Jesus get into the fishing boat? Why do you think Jesus brought so many fish to Peter's net?*

## "Be made clean"
### *Luke 5:12-16*

In one city was a man covered with leprosy. When he saw Jesus, he bowed to the ground. "If you choose," he begged, "you can make me clean."

"I do choose this," Jesus said. "Be made clean." Instantly the leprosy was gone. Jesus ordered him to tell no one. "Show the priest and make an offering to God."

But more than ever the news about Jesus spread. People were amazed when they heard him. Crowds would gather to listen and be healed of disease. Sometimes Jesus would get away to secluded places and pray.

*Questions: What did Jesus tell the healed leper to do? What did Jesus do when he got away from the crowds?*

# The Power to Forgive Sins
## Luke 5:17-26

Pharisees and teachers came from every village in Galilee. They came all the way from Jerusalem to Capernaum. Jesus was teaching them and God's power was with him to heal. Just then men came carrying a paralyzed man on a bed. They tried to bring him in the house to Jesus. But it was too crowded. So they went up on the roof and took off some roof tiles. They let the paralyzed man down into the house. There he was in front of Jesus in the middle of the crowd.

Jesus saw that these men had faith. "Friend," he said, "your sins are forgiven you."

The Pharisees questioned this. "He's speaking heresy," they whispered. "No one can forgive sins except God."

Jesus knew their thoughts. "Why do you question this? Is it easier to say: 'Your sins are forgiven,' or 'Stand up and walk?' I want you to know that I have the power to forgive sins." Then Jesus spoke to the paralyzed man: "Stand up, take your bed and go home." And the man did this, praising God.

Everyone was amazed and praised God. "We've seen great things today," they said.

*Questions: Why did the men let the paralyzed man down through the roof? What did the Pharisees say when Jesus forgave the man's sin?*

31

# Jesus Ignores the Sabbath
## Part One
### John 5:1-18

Jesus went up to the Passover festival. There, near the sheep gate, is a pool called Bethesda. Many blind, lame and paralyzed people waited there for the water to bubble up because of its healing power.

Jesus asked a man who'd been sick for thirty-eight years if he wanted to be made well.

"Someone always gets into the pool ahead of me."

Jesus said, "Stand up, take your mat, and walk." Instantly, the man was healed, picked up his mat, and walked.

Someone said, "Today's the sabbath. It's against the law to carry that mat."

"The man who healed me said to pick up my mat."

"Who was that?" the Pharisees asked.

"I don't know."

Jesus had left the area. Later, when the man saw Jesus in the temple, he told the Pharisees and they harassed Jesus because of the sabbath healing.

"My Father works everyday, and so do I," Jesus replied. The Pharisees wanted to kill Jesus for this. He'd made himself the same as God.

*Questions: How did the healed man break the law? Why did the Pharisees want to kill Jesus?*

# Jesus Ignores the Sabbath
### Part Two
### Mark 3:1-6

Jesus went into the synagogue on the sabbath. There was a man who had a disabled hand. The people wondered if he would heal on the sabbath. Jesus asked them, "Is it against the law to do good on the sabbath? What about to do harm? Does your law allow me to save a life on the sabbath? How about to kill?" They didn't answer.

"Stretch out your hand," he said to the man. The hand was healed. Right away the Pharisees plotted with the Romans to destroy Jesus.

*Questions: What did Jesus ask the people? Did the Pharisees want to destroy Jesus because he healed the man or because he ignored the sabbath law?*

33

# Jesus Teaches on the Mountain
### Matthew 5:1-9

Jesus saw the huge crowds on the mountain; His disciples too, came to him and he taught them:

The poor in spirit are blessed because theirs is the kingdom of heaven.

The meek are blessed because they'll inherit the earth.

People who are hungry to do right are blessed because they'll be filled.

People who have mercy are blessed because they'll be given mercy.

The pure in heart are blessed because they'll see God.

Peacemakers are blessed because they'll be called children of God.

*Questions: What kind of people inherit the earth?*
*What kind of people are called children of God?*

34

# The Faith of a Centurion
## Luke 7:1-10

In Capernaum lived an officer of the Roman army. He was called a centurion because he led 100 men. As a Roman he was a foreigner in Israel. The Jews called foreigners and non-Jews, "gentiles." So this centurion was a gentile. He had a favorite servant who was nearly dying. The centurion sent for Jesus: "Ask him to come and heal my slave," he said.

"This centurion deserves your help," they told Jesus. "He loves our people and paid for the building of our synagogue."

Not far from the man's house, friends of the centurion met Jesus. "The centurion sent this message:" They said. "'Lord, don't trouble yourself. I don't deserve to have you in my house. If you simply speak the words, my servant will be healed. I'm like you Lord, someone else tells me what to do. Then I give orders to my soldiers and servants.'"

Jesus was amazed that the centurion said this. He spoke to the crowd, "I haven't found this kind of faith in all of Israel."

When the centurion's friends returned, the servant was healed.

*Questions: The Jewish leader said the man deserved Jesus' help. What did the centurion say? What did Jesus say about this man's faith?*

35

# The Funeral at Nain
### *Luke 7:11-16*

Jesus and his disciples went to the town of Nain. A large crowd followed. There, a funeral procession came out of the town's gate. A young man had died. His mother, a widow, followed his body, weeping. A large crowd from the town was there.

The Lord saw her and had pity. "Don't weep," he said and stopped the procession. Then he said, "Young man, I say to you, get up!" The man sat up and began to speak. Jesus gave him to his mother.

The crowds were afraid. "A great prophet has come to us," they declared.

*Questions: How did the Lord feel when he saw the widow weeping? What did the crowd say about Jesus?*

# Sins and Love
## Part One
### Luke 7:36-39

A Pharisee named Simon invited Jesus to supper. There, a woman came with a beautiful little jar of perfume. She was weeping at Jesus' feet. This was a well-known, sinful woman who lived in town. Jesus' feet were bathed in her tears. Then the woman dried them with her hair. As this sinful woman kissed Jesus' feet, she anointed them with perfume.

"I don't think this man's a prophet." Simon said to himself. "If he were, he'd know who's touching him. She's a sinner."

*Questions: What did the woman do when she came to Jesus? What kind of woman was she?*

37

# Sins and Love
## Part Two
### Luke 7:40-50

Jesus spoke up. "Simon, I want to tell you a story."

"Two people owed another man money. The first owed 500 dollars. The other owed 50 dollars. Neither of them could pay. So he told them both they didn't need to pay him back. Which one loved him more?"

Simon the Pharisee answered, "I suppose the one who owed the most money."

Jesus said to him, "You're right. I came to your house. Did you give me water to wash my feet? No. Do you see this woman, Simon? She bathed my feet in tears and wiped them with her hair. You didn't greet me with a kiss. But since I came she hasn't stopped kissing my feet. You didn't anoint my head with oil. But she has anointed my feet. I tell you, her many sins are forgiven. But the one who's done little to forgive, loves little.

Jesus said to the woman, "Your sins are forgiven."

The people around the table murmured. "Who's this who forgives sins?"

And he said to the woman, "Your faith has saved you; go in peace."

Questions: Who had more sins, Simon the Pharisee or the weeping woman? Which one loved Jesus more?

# The Seeds of God's Word
## Luke 8:4-15

A great crowd gathered, and Jesus taught them with a story: "A farmer was planting seeds. As he spread the seeds, some fell on the path. Birds ate these seeds. Some seeds fell in with rocks. They died because there wasn't enough water. Seeds fell into the weeds and couldn't grow. Others fell into good soil. These seeds grew and gave the farmer a good crop."

Later, Jesus told his disciples, "The seeds are God's word. The ones that fell on the path mean this: Some people hear God's word. Then the devil takes it from their heart. So they can't believe and be saved.

"The seeds in the rocks are the people who happily believe for a little while. But in hard times, they forget God's word.

"The seeds in the weeds mean this: Some people hear God's word and go on their way. The word can't grow because their heart is full of other things.

"Then there are the seeds in good soil. These show God's word in a good heart. That person's life is changed forever."

*Questions: What are the farmer's seeds in this story? What happens when God's word comes into an honest heart?*

# The Wind and the Sea Obey Him
## Mark 4:35-5:6

At evening, Jesus said, "Let's cross to the other side." With other boats, the disciples rowed across the Sea of Galilee. A big storm came up. Waves beat into the boat. It was about to be swamped. But Jesus was asleep in the stern of the boat.

They awakened him. "Teacher, don't you care that we're all about to drown?"

He woke up and rebuked the wind. Speaking to the sea, Jesus said, "Peace! Be still." The wind stopped, and there was dead calm on the water.

"Why are you afraid?" He asked them. "Do you still have no faith?"

They were filled with great awe. "Who is this?" they asked each other. "Even the wind and the sea obey him."

They came to the other side of the sea. This was the country of the Gerasenes. A man lived in a graveyard here. He howled on the mountainsides and bruised himself with stones. An unclean spirit lived in this man. Whenever he was captured and chained, he broke the chains and escaped.

This man with an unclean spirit saw Jesus arrive at the shore.

*Questions: What did Jesus say about the disciples' faith? How did the disciples feel after Jesus calmed the sea?*

40

# The Man of Unclean Spirits
## Mark 5:6-20

The man with the unclean spirit spied Jesus. He screamed and shouted: "What do you have to do with me? Jesus, Son of the Most High God!"

"Come out of him, you unclean spirit!" Jesus commanded.

"I beg you in God's name, don't make me suffer," it answered.

"What's your name," Jesus asked the spirit.

"It's Legion because there are many of us in this man. Please, don't send us away."

Nearby grazed a herd of pigs. "Let us enter into the pigs," the spirits begged. Jesus gave them permission. The legion of spirits came out of the man, entering the pigs, and all the animals rushed down the hill and into the sea.

People found the man of unclean spirits fully clothed and sitting in his right mind with Jesus. They were afraid and pleaded with Jesus, "Go away!"

Before leaving, Jesus spoke to the man, "Go home. Tell your friends how much the Lord has done for you." The man went to ten cities telling what Jesus had done.

*Questions: What happened when the spirits entered the pigs? What did the man who had the spirits do after Jesus left?*

# "Who touched me?"
### Mark 5:22-34

Again they crossed the sea in the boat. On the other shore a big crowd gathered. A Jewish leader named Jairus came forward and fell at his feet. "My little daughter is about to die. Come and touch her so she will live." So Jesus went with him. The crowd followed and pushed in on him.

In the crowd was a woman who'd been bleeding for twelve years. She had spent all her money on doctors. They couldn't help her; in fact, she grew worse. She'd heard about Jesus and came up behind him. She said to herself, "If I touch his clothes, I'll be healed." She touched his cloak. Instantly her bleeding stopped. The woman knew she was healed.

Jesus also knew something had happened. He had felt power go out from him. "Who touched me?" he asked.

"The crowd is pushing in on you," said his disciples. "How can you ask, 'Who touched me?'" But he looked all around for who had done it.

The woman came to him in fear and trembling. She told him the whole story. "Daughter," he said, "your faith has made you well. Go in peace and be healed."

*Questions: What happened to Jesus when the woman touched him? What did Jesus say had made her well?*

42

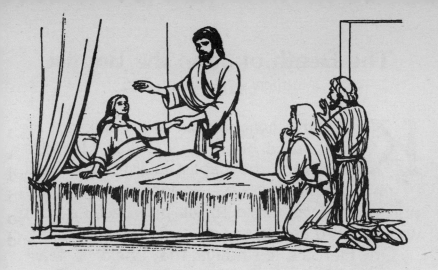

# "She's not dead; she's sleeping"
### Mark 5:35-43

"Your daughter's dead, Jairus," people said. "Don't trouble the teacher." But Jesus overheard.

"Don't fear, Jairus," he said. "Only believe."

Jesus wouldn't let anyone follow him to Jairus' house. Only Peter, James and John went along. There, people loudly wailed.

"Why so much noise? She's not dead; she's sleeping." They laughed at Jesus. He put them outside. With her parents and the disciples, Jesus went to the girl. He took her hand. "Little girl, get up." She arose and walked around. They were overcome with amazement. "Don't tell anyone," Jesus ordered. "And give her something to eat."

*Questions: What did Jesus tell Jairus to do? What did the people do when Jesus came to the house?*

# The Death of John the Baptist
## Matthew 14:1-12; 11:7-15

King Herod was wicked and confused. He had married his brother's wife, Herodias. When John the Baptist heard this he said, "That's against the law." So Herod put John in prison. He was afraid to kill him because John was honored as a prophet.

On Herod's birthday, they held a feast. Herodias' daughter danced and Herod was happy with her. "I'll give you anything you want," he promised.

Her mother told her, "Ask for John the Baptist's head on a plate." And she did. The king was troubled about this. But everyone had heard his promise. So he sent guards to cut off John's head. It was given to the girl who gave it to Herodias.

Jesus had talked to his disciples about John: "He was more than a prophet. He is the man the prophet Malachi wrote about: 'Look, I'm sending my messenger ahead of you. He will prepare a way for you.' John did this for me.

"No one ever born was greater than John the Baptist. But the littlest in the kingdom of heaven is greater than he is. He heard that the good news was coming. Now the good news is yours."

*Questions: What did John the Baptist do for Jesus? Why are the littlest in the kingdom greater than John?*

# Jesus Feeds the Crowds
### Matthew 14:13-18

Jesus heard John the Baptist had been killed. So he retreated in a boat to a secluded place. The people followed on foot around the Sea of Galilee. So when Jesus came ashore, he saw huge crowds waiting. There he cared for them.

"It's late," said the disciples. "Send them away for food."

"They don't need to leave," said Jesus. "You give them food."

"All we have is five loaves and two fish."

Taking these Jesus looked up to heaven. He blessed and broke the loaves. Then everyone ate their fill. They filled twelve baskets with leftovers.

*Questions: Why did the disciples want to send the people away? What did Jesus want the disciples to do?*

45

# Jesus Walks on the Sea
### Matthew 14:22-36

After feeding the crowds, Jesus sent the disciples back to the boat. He went up the mountain alone to pray. By evening the boat was far from land. The disciples struggled to sail against high waves and strong winds. At dawn Jesus came to them walking on the sea.

"It's a ghost!" they cried out in fear.

"Take heart, it is I," Jesus said. "Don't be afraid."

Peter answered, "Lord, command me to walk on the water."

He said, "Come."

So Peter started walking on the water toward Jesus. But when Peter saw the wind he began sink, Peter cried out, "Lord, save me!"

Instantly Jesus reached and caught him. "You have so little faith," Jesus said. "Why did you doubt?" Back in the boat, the wind stopped.

"Truly you are the Son of God," they said. And the disciples worshiped him.

When the boat came to land, the sick were brought to Jesus. "Just let us touch the edge of your cloak," the people begged. All those who touched it were healed.

*Questions: What did the disciples think when Jesus came walking on the sea? Why did Peter begin to sink?*

46

# Jesus—The Bread of Life
### John 6:25-68

Jesus told the crowd, "You want me because I fed you yesterday. But hunger for food that gives you eternal life. I'll give you this food."

"What good works can we do for God?" they asked.

"Believe in the one that God has sent."

They said, "when we see a miracle we'll believe in you. Our ancestors ate manna from heaven. What are you going to do for us?"

"My Father has given you real bread from heaven. God's bread is the one he's sent to give the world life."

"Sir," they pleaded, "always give us this bread."

Then Jesus said to them, "I'm the bread of life. Whoever comes to me will never be hungry. Whoever believes in me will never be thirsty.

"Your ancestors ate the manna, and still they died. I'm the living bread that came down from heaven. Whoever eats this bread will live forever."

Some of his disciples complained about this teaching and left him.

"Will you leave too?" Jesus asked.

"Where will we go?" answered Peter. "You have the words of eternal life."

*Questions: The crowds wanted to work for God. What did Jesus say they should do? Who is the real bread?*

# A Gentile Dog and
# the Bread of Life
### Matthew 15:21-31

Leaving Capernaum and traveling north, Jesus came to Tyre and Sidon, a place where gentiles lived. A Canaanite women shouted, "Have mercy on me, Lord, Son of David! My daughter is harassed by a demon."

His disciples urged him, "Send her away."

She came and knelt down. "Lord, help me."

"It wouldn't be fair," he answered. "I can't throw Israel's bread to the gentile dogs."

"That's true, Lord," she said. "But little dogs get the crumbs that fall from their masters' table."

"Woman, you have great faith! You may have what you wish." And her daughter was healed instantly.

After this Jesus journeyed back along the Sea of Galilee. He went up a mountainside and sat down. Huge crowds came with the lame, the blind, the mute, and others. They were brought to him, and he cured them. The crowd was amazed. They saw the mute speaking, the lame walking, and the blind seeing. And they praised the God of Israel.

*Questions: At first, Jesus wouldn't help the woman. Why? What did the woman say that showed Jesus she had faith?*

48

# "Who do people say I am?"
### Matthew 16:13-23

At Caesarea Philippi, Jesus asked his disciples, "Who do people say I am?"

"Some say you're John the Baptist. Others say Elijah. Still others think you're Jeremiah or one of the prophets."

He said to them, "Who do you say that I am?"

Peter spoke up. "You're the Christ, the Son of the living God."

"You're blessed, Peter," said Jesus. "No man told you this. My Father in heaven has shown it to you. This is the rock on which I'll build my church. You, Peter, are a stone in that building. And the church I'll build is stronger than the gates of Hell." He sternly told them, "Don't tell anyone I'm the Christ."

He began to tell his disciples what would soon happen: "I'll go to Jerusalem. There I'll suffer and be killed. Three days later, I'll return from death."

"God forbid it, Lord," declared Peter. "This must never happen to you!"

Jesus rebuked Peter. "If you think that way you'll block my plans. Your words are from Satan. You see me as a human king. Instead, you must understand: God sent me so that these things could happen."

*Questions: Who did Peter say Jesus was? What was going to happen to Jesus in Jerusalem?*

# The Voice on the Mountaintop
### *Matthew 17:1-8*

Six days later Jesus took Peter, James, and John to the mountaintop. There Jesus was changed. His face shone like the sun. His clothes became dazzling. Suddenly, Moses and Elijah appeared and spoke with Jesus.

Peter said, "Shall we pitch three tents? One to worship you, one to worship Moses, and one for Elijah?" Peter was talking when a bright cloud covered them.

A voice spoke from the cloud, "This is my beloved Son. He pleases me. Listen to him!" The disciples fell to the ground in fear. When they looked up, only Jesus was there.

*Questions: What did Peter want to do when he saw Jesus changed? What did God want Peter to do?*

# Nothing is Impossible with Faith
### Matthew 17:14-21

Jesus and the three disciples came down the mountain to the crowd. A man knelt down in front of Jesus. "Lord, have mercy on my son. An evil spirit controls him; he suffers terribly. Sometimes he falls into the fire. Other times he falls into the water. I brought him to your disciples, but they couldn't cure him."

Jesus said, "You people have no faith. You're so corrupt. How much longer do I have to put up with you? Bring the boy to me." Jesus rebuked the demon and it came out. The boy was cured instantly.

The disciples took him aside and asked, "Why couldn't we do that?"

"Because you have so little faith. You could do so much with just a tiny bit of faith. Faith the size of a mustard seed can move a mountain into the sea. With faith, nothing would be impossible for you."

They were all living in Galilee. There Jesus told them, "I am going to be trapped and sold to men in Jerusalem. They will kill me. Three days later I'll return from death." These words upset and worried the disciples.

*Questions: Why couldn't the disciples cure the boy?*
*Why were the disciples worried about Jesus?*

# The Greatest in the Kingdom
### Matthew 17:24-8:5

In Capernaum, the time had come to collect the temple tax. The tax collectors came to Peter. "Does Jesus pay the tax?" they asked.

"Yes, he does," Peter answered.

When Peter came home Jesus asked him this question: "From whom do kings collect taxes? Do they take the money from their own children or from others?"

"From others," Peter answered.

"Then the king's children don't pay the temple tax. However, we don't want to trouble the tax collectors. Go to the sea and cast in a hook. Pull in the first fish you hook. When you open its mouth you'll find a coin. Take that and give it to them. It will pay your tax and mine."

Then the disciples asked Jesus a question: "Which of us·will be greatest in the kingdom of heaven?"

Jesus called to a little child. "I'll tell you the truth. Do you want to enter the kingdom? Then you'll have to change and become like a little child. Anyone who is humble like this child is greatest in the kingdom. Anyone who welcomes such a child, welcomes me."

*Questions: Why would Jesus not have to pay the temple tax? What kind of person enters into the kingdom of heaven?*

# "Forgive others from your heart"
### Matthew 18:21-35

Peter asked, "How often should I forgive someone? Seven times?"

Jesus answered, "Not seven times, I tell you: seventy-seven times.

"Once a king's servant owed him ten million dollars. He couldn't pay. The king ordered, 'Sell this man and his family into slavery to pay his debt.'

"The servant begged, 'Be patient. I'll pay you everything.' Pitying him, he said, 'You don't have to pay.'

"Later, a man owed him 100 dollars. 'Pay me what you owe,' he demanded. The man pleaded, 'Have patience. I'll pay you!' But the servant put him in jail until he could pay.

"Other servants saw this and told the king. The king said to the servant, 'You wicked servant. I forgave you your debt because you begged me to. I had mercy on you. Shouldn't you have had mercy on that man?' The king sent him to prison until he'd paid his debt.

"Peter, the lesson is this: My Father is like the king in this story. You are like the servant. So always forgive others from your heart."

*Questions: Peter wanted to forgive seven times. How many times did Jesus say to forgive? What is the lesson of Jesus' story?*

# The Camel in the Needle's Eye
### Matthew 19:16-26

A young man asked, "What shall I do to have eternal life?"

"Keep the commandments," Jesus answered.

"I've kept all ten. What else is there?"

"Sell everything. Give the money to the poor. Come and follow me."

When the young man heard this, he sadly walked away. He was very rich.

Jesus spoke to his disciples: "Can a camel go through a needle's eye? That's how hard it is for the rich to enter the kingdom."

"So who can be saved?" they wondered.

"To you it's impossible," he answered. "But God can do anything."

*Questions: What did the young man want? What did the young man want to keep?*

54

# The One Thing That's Needed
*Luke 10:38-42*

One day Jesus went to Martha and Mary's house. Mary had once anointed Jesus' feet and wiped them with her hair. She enjoyed sitting at the Lord's feet listening to him talk. Martha was very busy with other things in the house. She asked Jesus, "My sister has left all the work for me to do. Does that bother you at all?"

"Martha, Martha," he answered, "you're worried about so many things. But there's only one thing that's really needed. Mary has chosen to love me, and that won't be taken from her."

*Questions: What was Martha bothered about? What was the one thing that Mary had chosen?*

55

# Mud on a Blind Man's Eyes
## Part One
### John 9:1-9

As Jesus walked in Jerusalem, he saw a blind man. This man had been born blind. His disciples asked this question: "Teacher, whose fault was it that he is blind? Did his parents sin? Was it his sin that caused this?"

"He was born blind for a reason," Jesus answered. "This has nothing to do with anyone's sin. God wants to work in him. We must do God's work while it is day. Night is coming when no one can work. As long as I'm in the world, I'm the light of the world."

Then Jesus spit on the ground. He made mud with his spit and spread it on the man's eyes. "Go wash your eyes in the Siloam pool," Jesus told him.

The blind man went to the pool with mud on his eyes. He washed and for the first time in his life he could see. His neighbors had always seen him begging. "Isn't this the man who used to sit and beg?" they asked.

"It's the same man," some said.

"No," others said. "This man just looks like him."

He told them, "I'm the same man."

*Questions: What was the reason the man was blind? When Jesus was in the world, what was he?*

# Mud on a Blind Man's Eyes
## Part Two
### John 9:10-25

The once-blind beggar tried to explain why he could see: "Jesus spread the mud on my eyes and said 'wash at Siloam Pool.'"

Because it was the Sabbath, they brought the man to the Pharisees. "This man isn't from God," some Pharisees said.

"But how could a sinner do this miracle?" others asked. The Pharisees couldn't agree. So they asked the blind beggar, "What do you think? He gave you your sight."

"He's a prophet."

The Pharisees didn't believe him. "He was never blind," they said. So they asked his parents.

"This is our son," they said. "He was born blind. We don't know why he can now see. He's a grown man. Ask him." So the Pharisees called the man for the second time.

"You should only praise God that you can see," they said. "Jesus made mud on the sabbath. He's a sinner, not a miracle worker."

"I don't know if he's a sinner," the man answered. "I do know that once I was blind. Now I see."

Questions: Why did they bring the man to the Pharisees? Why did the Pharisees say that Jesus was a sinner?

# Mud on a Blind Man's Eyes
## Part Three
### John 9:26-41

"I already told you, Jesus gave me my sight," said the once-blind beggar. "Do you want to be his follower like me?"

The Pharisees cursed him. "You follow Jesus But we're followers of Moses. We know that God spoke to Moses. But we don't know where Jesus comes from."

"This is amazing!" exclaimed the man. "You don't know where he comes from? He opened my eyes! Everybody knows that God doesn't listen to sinners. God listens to those who worship and obey him. Since the world began, no one born blind could see. If Jesus weren't from God he couldn't do this."

"You were born a sinner," said the Pharisees "Do you think you can teach us?" They threw him out. "You can't be a Jew anymore."

Jesus heard they'd thrown the man out. Jesus went looking for him. He found the man and asked, "Do you believe in the Son of God?"

"Who is he sir?"

"You've seen him. He's speaking with you right now," Jesus answered.

"Lord, I believe." and the man worshiped Jesus

*Questions: Who does God listen to? What happened to the man because he followed Jesus?*

# Jesus—The Good Shepherd
## John 10:1-39

" A shepherd keeps his sheep safe in a barn. The shepherd always goes into the barn through the door. A thief sneaks into the barn another way. The shepherd knows his sheep by name, and they know his voice. They won't follow a stranger."

Jesus was explaining why the once-blind man followed him. But the people couldn't understand his meaning. So he tried again: "This is the truth. I'm the barn door. All who came before me are thieves. But the sheep didn't listen to them. Remember, I'm the door. Anyone who enters through me will be saved. They'll go in and out of the pasture. The thieves come to kill. I came that people would have life, overflowing life.

"I'm the good shepherd. The good shepherd gives his life for the sheep. I know my own sheep and my sheep know me. Just like the Father knows me and I know my Father."

"You're only human. God isn't your father!" Some of the Jews picked up stones to throw at Jesus.

"I've done many of my Father's good works. Is this why you want to stone me?" When they tried to arrest Jesus, he escaped.

*Questions: Why did Jesus come? Why did some people want to throw stones at Jesus?*

# Lambs Among Wolves
### Luke 10:1-24

Jesus sent out seventy disciples, in pairs to every town that he would soon visit. "There's a harvest of people out there," he told them. "Pray the Lord of the harvest for more laborers.

"I send you like lambs among wolves. Don't carry a backpack or money or extra shoes. When you go into someone's house say, 'Peace to this house.' When people welcome you to town, eat the food they offer. Cure their sick. Tell them, 'The kingdom of God has come near you.' Whoever listens to you listens to me. If they turn you away, they've turned me away."

The seventy apostles returned full of joy. "Lord, in your name even the evil spirits obey us!"

"Don't rejoice over this," He said. "Instead rejoice that your names are written in heaven."

Nearby stood a lawyer who knew the Jewish law. This man asked the Lord, "What should I do to get eternal life?"

"What does the law say?" asked Jesus.

Love God with your whole heart," answered the lawyer. And love your neighbor like you love yourself."

"That's right. Do this and you'll have life," said Jesus.

*Questions: What were the seventy apostles to say to people? Why should the apostles rejoice?*

# The Good Samaritan
### *Luke 10:30-37*

The lawyer wanted to trick Jesus. He asked, "Who is my neighbor?"

Jesus answered with a story: "A man traveled from Jerusalem to Jericho. He was robbed and beaten by bandits. As he lay on the road, a priest walked right by. So did a Levite. But a Samaritan had pity. He washed and bandaged the traveler's wounds and carried him to a nearby inn. This Samaritan paid the innkeeper to care for the man.

"Which of these three were the wounded man's neighbor?"

"The man who had pity."

"Right," said Jesus. "Go and do the same."

*Questions: Who didn't help the wounded traveler? Who had pity on the traveler?*

# Jesus is the Resurrection

### Part One
### John 11:17-24

A man named Lazarus lay sick in Bethany, Mary's and Martha's village. These women sent a message to Jesus: "Lazarus is sick." But when Jesus heard this, he waited two days. Then Jesus said to the disciples, "Let's go back to Judea."

"But teacher," they said, "people want to kill you there."

"Our friend Lazarus has fallen asleep," he said. "I'm going to awaken him."

"Well Lord, if he's only asleep he'll be fine." Jesus meant that Lazarus was dead. The disciples didn't understand this.

When Jesus got to Bethany, Lazarus had been dead four days. Martha went out to meet Jesus while Mary stayed home. "Lord, if you'd been here," she said, "Lazarus wouldn't have died. But I know God will give you anything you ask."

"Your brother will return from death."

"I know, Lord," said Martha. "He'll come back with the resurrection on the last day."

Questions: What did the disciples think would happen if Jesus went to Judea? When did Martha think Lazarus would return from death?

# Jesus is the Resurrection
### Part Two
### John 11:25-38

"I am the resurrection and the life," said Jesus to Martha. "Those who believe in me may die, but they'll live again. Do you believe this, Martha?"

"Yes, Lord." Martha replied. "I believe you're Christ, God's Son who's come into the world." Then she hurried home.

"Mary," whispered Martha, "the Teacher is here. He wants to see you." The Jews saw Mary leave and followed her. They thought she was going to Lazarus' tomb to weep. But they found her kneeling at Jesus' feet.

"Lord, you should have been here," Mary wept. "Then Lazarus wouldn't have died." Jesus saw her weeping. He looked up and saw all her Jewish friends weeping. This troubled him.

"Where did you bury him?"

"Come and see, Lord."

Jesus began to weep. "See how much he loved Lazarus," some said.

But others said, "He made the blind man see. Couldn't he have kept this man from dying?" These words made Jesus sad.

*Questions: Jesus said he was the resurrection and the life. What did Martha think that meant? What did the people say that made Jesus sad?*

# Jesus is the Resurrection

*Part Three*
*John 11:38-53*

L azarus' tomb was covered by a boulder. "Remove it," he said.

"Lord," complained Martha, "the body's begun to stink."

"Martha, I told you to believe and you'd see God's glory. Thank you, Father. You've heard me." Jesus said this so the people would believe in him. He spoke loudly: "Lazarus, come out."

Many Jews saw Lazarus come forth and believed. Others told the Pharisees who worried, "Soon everyone will believe in him." So they plotted to kill Jesus.

*Questions: Why didn't Martha want to take the stone from Lazarus' tomb? Why did the Pharisees plot to kill Jesus?*

# Set Free on the Sabbath
### Luke 13:10-17

The Lord was teaching at a synagogue on the sabbath. Into the room walked a woman controlled by a crippling spirit. She'd been bent over for eighteen years. She had no way to stand up straight. Jesus saw her and called her over. "Woman," he said, "you're set free from your disability." He touched her with his hands. Instantly she stood up straight and praised God.

But the leader of the synagogue was furious. Jesus had cured the woman on the sabbath. It was against the law to work on the sabbath. The leader spoke to the crowd: "There are six days in the week to work. Come on those days to be cured, not on the sabbath."

The Lord answered him, "You faker. You all untie your donkey on the sabbath. Then you lead it away to give it water. This woman is a daughter of Abraham. Satan has crippled her for eighteen long years. Shouldn't she be set free from this on the sabbath?"

When he said this all his enemies were put to shame. The entire crowd rejoiced to see the wonderful things he did.

*Questions: Why was the leader of the synagogue furious? Why did the Lord call him a faker?*

65

# God's Search for Sinners
## Part One
### *Luke 15:1-13*

Tax collectors and sinners gathered to hear Jesus. Pharisees and other religious people grumbled: "Jesus welcomes sinners and even eats with them."

So Jesus told them this story: "Suppose you have a hundred sheep and lose one. Don't you leave the ninety-nine to search for the lost sheep? When you find it you return with joy. You say to your friends, 'Rejoice with me! I've found my lost sheep.' So listen to me. There's great joy in heaven when one sinner turns away from sin. Much more than over ninety-nine lawkeepers like you."

*Questions: Why were the Pharisees grumbling? When is there joy in heaven?*

# God's Search for Sinners
## Part Two
### Luke 15:13-24

Jesus thought this story would help them:
"A man had two sons. He divided his property between them. The younger son took his share and went to a far away country. He spent everything he had there in foolish living. Then famine came to the land. With no food he worked feeding pigs. He had to eat the pigs' food.

"At last he started thinking sensibly. 'My father's servants have food. But here I am starving! I'm going home. I'll say, 'Father, I've sinned against heaven and against you. Don't call me your son anymore. Make me one of your hired workers.'

"He set off for home. His father saw him coming. Filled with love, he ran and hugged his son. The young man said, 'Father, I've sinned against you. I shouldn't be called your son anymore.' But his father interrupted.

"'Quickly,' the father told his servants, 'bring my best clothes for him. Put a ring on his finger and shoes on his feet. Let's eat and celebrate! My son was dead and now he's alive. He was lost and now he's found.' They began to celebrate."

*Questions: What did the young man think his father should do when he returned? What did the father do instead?*

# God's Search for Sinners
## Part Three
### Luke 15:25-32

"You lawkeepers should know about the father's older son." Jesus continued. "Hearing music, he asked what was happening. "'Your brother has come home safe and sound. So your father is giving a feast for him.'

"The older son was angry. So his father came out and asked him to come and celebrate.

"'Listen,' the son answered, 'I've been working for you for years. I've worked like a slave and never disobeyed. But I've not even had a little party with my friends. Now this son of yours comes back. He's wasted your property in sin. And you throw a huge feast!'

"'Son,' answered the father, 'you're always with me. Everything that's mine is yours. We must celebrate and rejoice. Your brother was dead and has come to life. He was lost and has been found.'"

Remember that the Pharisees had grumbled because Jesus ate with sinners. He told these stories so they would understand why he did this. Jesus hoped the lawkeepers would see why God loves sinners.

*Questions: Why was the older son angry at the father? What did the father say to the older son that showed he loved him too?*

# Lazarus and the Rich Man
## Luke 16:19-31

Jesus told another story:
"A rich man had fine clothes and excellent food. Another man, Lazarus, was covered with sores and begged for scraps in the street. Dogs licked his sores.

"Lazarus died. Angels carried him to Abraham.

"The rich man died and was in torment. Far away he saw Abraham with Lazarus at his side. He called, 'Father Abraham, have mercy. Send Lazarus with a drop of water to cool my tongue. I'm in agony in these flames.'

"'Child,' answered Abraham, 'remember, in life you had good things. Lazarus had evil. Now he's comfortable and you're suffering. No one can come back.'

"'Father,' said the rich man, 'Send Lazarus to warn my brothers. Then they won't have to suffer like me.'

"'They should listen to the words of Moses and the prophets.'

"'No, Father Abraham. If someone comes from the dead, then they'll listen.'

"'They don't listen to Moses. If someone comes back from death they won't listen to him either.'"

*Questions: Why wouldn't Abraham send Lazarus to the rich man's brothers? Why wouldn't the rich man's brothers listen to Lazarus?*

# The Humble and the Honored
## Luke 18:1-14

This story is to inspire people to always pray: "There was a judge who didn't fear God or respect people. He refused to be fair to a widow. But she came back to him again and again. 'By law, you must be fair in this matter,' she said.

Finally the judge said, 'I don't respect anyone. But this widow's a bother. So I'll be fair in her case. Her demands will soon wear me out.'

"Pay attention to what this unfair judge said. Now, don't you think God will be fair when you pray? Will he wait? No. He'll act quickly. Yet when I return, will I find people praying in faith?"

Then he told another story. It's for people who think they're pure and look down on others:

"A Pharisee and a tax collector were praying. The Pharisee stood and prayed: 'Thank you I'm not like that tax collector. I always perform my religious duty.' Far away the tax collector wouldn't even look up to heaven. In grief he prayed: 'Have mercy on me. I'm a sinner.'

"Listen, God accepted him, not the Pharisee. Praise yourself and you'll be humbled. Humble yourself and you'll be honored."

*Questions: What does Jesus want to find when he returns? What will happen if you praise yourself?*

70

# "Let the little children come"
### Luke 18:15-17

Parents brought their children and tiny babies to Jesus. They only wanted him to touch them. But then the disciples noticed what these parents were doing. They sternly ordered them to stop.

But Jesus called for them, "Let the little children come to me. Don't stop them. The kingdom of God belongs to people like these children.

"I'll tell you the truth: You must receive the kingdom like a child. If not, you will never enter into it." Then he held the babies and gently touched the children.

*Questions: Who does God's kingdom belong to? What do you need to be like to enter the kingdom?*

# "Your faith has saved you"
## Luke 18:35-43

Blind Bartimaeus sat by the Jericho road begging. "Jesus is walking by," someone said. "Jesus, Son of David," Bartimaeus shouted. "Have mercy on me!" The people in front sternly ordered him to be quiet. But Bartimaeus only shouted louder: "Son of David, have mercy on me!" Jesus stopped and ordered the man to be brought to him.

"What do you want me to do for you?"

"Lord, let me see again."

"Receive your sight," said Jesus. "Your faith has saved you." Instantly Bartimaeus could see. He followed Jesus praising God with all the people.

*Questions: What name did Bartimaeus call Jesus? What saved Bartimaeus?*

72

# "Salvation has come to this house"
### Luke 19:1-28

Bartimaeus and the crowd followed Jesus into Jericho. As he was passing through more people gathered to see him. A man was there named Zacchaeus. He was a rich man because he was in charge of tax collecting. He was trying to see Jesus. But Zacchaeus was too short to see over the crowd. So he ran ahead to a sycamore tree. He climbed the tree to see over the people. Jesus was going to pass that way. Jesus came there, looked up, and said, "Zacchaeus, hurry down. I'm going to stay at your house today."

So Zacchaeus hurried down and happily welcomed Jesus to his house. But people grumbled, "Jesus is a guest in the house of a sinner."

Zacchaeus stood there in his house. "Lord," he said, "half of all I own I'll give to the poor. If I've cheated anyone, I'll pay them back four times as much."

"Today, salvation has come to this house." Jesus spoke to everyone within earshot. "Zacchaeus is a son of Abraham just as you are. Remember, the Son of Man came to seek out and save the lost."

*Questions: Why did the people grumble? Why did Jesus, the Son of Man, come?*

# "What a waste!"

### Matthew 26:6-13

Jesus stayed in Bethany. A woman came with a little jar of expensive perfume. She poured it on Jesus' head as he sat at the table. The disciples were angry. "What a waste!" they said. "We could have sold it and given the money to the poor."

"Don't trouble her." Jesus said. "She's done a good thing. You always have poor people with you. I won't always be here. She's prepared my body for burial. Listen: The gospel will be preached all over the world. Then, what this woman has done for me will be remembered."

*Questions: The woman poured the perfume on Jesus. What did the disciples want to do with it? When is this story remembered?*

# "Your king is humbly coming"
### Matthew 21:1-11; Luke 19:29-35

While Jesus was in Bethany, Judas, one of the disciples, went into Jerusalem. There he spoke with the leading priests: "What will you give if I betray Jesus to you?" They paid Judas thirty pieces of silver. From that moment, he looked for a chance to double cross the Lord.

Meanwhile Jesus was headed for Jerusalem. "Go into the village ahead," He instructed two disciples. "You'll find a donkey and her colt that's never been ridden. Untie them and bring them to me. If anyone says anything to you, don't worry. Say, 'The Lord needs them.' He'll send them right away."

The two disciples found it just as he said. The owner asked them, "Why are you untying the donkey?" They said, "The Lord needs it." Then they brought him the donkey and her colt. They spread their cloaks over the animals' backs. Jesus rode the donkey from the Mount of Olives into Jerusalem.

Long before Jesus was born, Zechariah the prophet said this would happen. He wrote: "Look Zion, your king is humbly coming to you. He's riding on a donkey and on a donkey's colt."

*Questions: How much was Judas paid to betray Jesus? What did Zechariah say about Jesus' ride into Jerusalem?*

# "Hosanna in the highest heaven!"
## Luke 19:36-44

Jesus rode down the Mount of Olives. People covered the path with their cloaks. Others spread palm leaves in the way. They praised God loudly and joyfully: "Blessed is the king who comes in the name of the Lord! Hosanna in the highest heaven!"

Some of the Pharisees said, "Teacher, order your disciples to stop."

He answered, "I tell you, if they were silent, the stones would shout."

Then Jesus saw Jerusalem and wept. "Your enemies will tear you down, stone by stone," he said. "Because you didn't notice the day God visited you."

*Questions: What did Jesus say would happen if the people were silent? Why did Jesus weep when he saw Jerusalem?*

# The House of Prayer
### Matthew 21:12-17; Mark 11:15-19

Jesus went to the temple in Jerusalem and drove out the people buying and selling and upset their money tables. People were there selling doves for sacrifices. Jesus knocked over their chairs. Then he announced: "This is written in the Scriptures: 'My house will be called a house of prayer; but you are making it a den of robbers.'"

The leading priests heard what he'd done. They kept looking for a way to kill Jesus. But they were afraid of him. The whole crowd was spellbound by his teaching.

The blind and disabled came to him in the temple. He cured them. The leading priests saw these amazing things. They heard the children joyfully shouting in the temple: "Hosanna to the Son of David!" This made the priests angry. "Do you hear what these children are saying?" they asked him.

"Yes," Jesus answered. "Haven't you ever read in the Scripture: Praise has come from the mouths of infants and nursing babies. You've prepared this praise for yourself?" Then he left for Bethany to spend the night.

*Questions: God wanted the temple to be a house of prayer. What had it become? Why were the priests afraid of Jesus?*

77

# The Story of the Vineyard
## Matthew 21:33-46

Jesus told another story:

"A man planted a vineyard and built a winery there. He then rented the vineyard and went into another country. At harvest, the servants arrived to collect his share of fruit. But the renters beat one servant. They killed another and stoned a third. The man sent more servants but they were treated the same. Finally he sent his son. 'They'll respect my son,' the man thought.

"'Here comes the owner's son,' said the renters. 'Someday this vineyard will be his. Let's kill him. Then the land will be ours.' So they tackled him and killed him.

"Answer this:" continued Jesus. "When the owner comes, what will he do to those renters?"

"He'll put those villains to death," they answered. "He'll rent the vineyard to people who'll give him the fruit on time."

"Right," said Jesus. "So God's kingdom will be taken away from you. It will be give to people who produce the kingdom's fruit."

The leading priests heard his story. They knew Jesus was talking about them and wanted to arrest him. But they couldn't because the people saw Jesus as a prophet.

*Questions: Who will be given God's kingdom? Why couldn't the priests arrest Jesus?*

# The Story of the Wedding Feast
### Matthew 22:1-14

Jesus told another story:
"A king gave a wedding feast for his son," he began. "He sent his servants to bring the invited guests. But they wouldn't come. So the king said, 'Tell them this: I've done everything. The wedding feast is ready; come and enjoy it.' But those he'd invited mocked the feast. They went away to their farms and businesses. Others hurt the king's servants and killed them.

"The king was enraged. His soldiers destroyed those murderers and burned their city. Then he told his servants, 'Go into the streets. Invite everyone to my son's wedding feast.' The servants invited the good and the bad people from the streets. The feast was filled with guests.

"The king came into the feast. He noticed a man who wasn't wearing wedding clothes. 'Friend,' he said, 'how did you get in without wedding clothes?' The man could say nothing. 'Tie him up,' commanded the king. 'Throw him out into the darkness. There people weep and grind their teeth with grief.'"

Jesus ended the story with this saying: "Many are called but few are chosen."

*Questions: What did the invited guests do instead of going to the feast? Who did the servants invite from the streets?*

# What to Give to God
*Matthew 22:15-22; Mark 12:41-44*

The Pharisees were in charge of the Jewish religion. But the Romans ruled the land. Some Pharisees and Romans wanted to trick Jesus. "Teacher, we know you teach God's way. Tell us, should we pay taxes to the Roman emperor?"

"Why are you testing me?" asked Jesus. "You're phonies. Show me a coin that you'd use to pay taxes." They brought him a Roman coin. "Whose picture and title are on this coin?" Jesus asked.

"The emperor's picture," they answered.

"Right. So give the emperor what belongs to him. And give God what belongs to God." They heard this and were amazed. All they could do was leave him alone.

Later Jesus taught his disciples more about giving to God. They were sitting near a room called the treasury. Here people brought gifts of money for the temple. Many rich people brought lots of money. A poor widow came with two pennies. Jesus said, "I'll tell you the truth. This widow has given more than all the others put together. They have plenty to give. She has nothing and has given everything she has."

*Questions: What did Jesus say we should give to God? Why was the widow's gift more than everyone else's?*

# The Story of the Ten Bridesmaids
*Matthew 24:1,2; 25:1-13*

Jesus' disciples said, "Teacher, look at these beautiful temple buildings."

Jesus replied, "Not one of their stones will be left upon another. All this will be destroyed."

The disciples asked, "When will this happen, Lord?" Jesus answered them with this story:

"Ten bridesmaids had their lamps and were waiting to meet the bridegroom. Five of them were foolish. Five were wise. The foolish ones had lamps but no extra oil. The wise had extra oil for their lamps.

"At midnight they heard a shout, 'The bridegroom is coming!' The bridesmaids lit their lamps. The foolish said to the wise, 'Give us some oil. Our lamps are going out.' But the others said, 'No, there's not enough for all of us. Go buy your own.'

"While they went to buy oil, the bridegroom arrived. He took the wise bridesmaids into the wedding feast. The door was shut. Then the other bridesmaids came. 'Lord, lord, open the door,' they called. The bridegroom answered, 'I don't know who you are.'"

"So be alert. You don't know the day or the hour when your Lord will come."

*Questions: What did Jesus say would happen to the temple? What can we learn from the story of the bridesmaids?*

# Jesus Tells of His Return
### Matthew 25:31-46

"When I come in glory, I'll sit on a glorious throne. All the nations on earth will gather there. I'll divide the people into two groups. This is like a shepherd who separates the sheep from the goats. I'll say to those on the right, 'Come here. You're blessed by my Father. Here's the kingdom he has waiting for you. I was hungry and you gave me food. I was thirsty, and you gave me something to drink. When I was a stranger, you welcomed me. I was naked and you gave me clothes. You visited me in prison.'

"Those people will ask, 'When did we do these things?'

"'Here's the truth: You did this to the smallest member of my family. So you did it to me.'

"Then I'll speak to those on my left side. 'Get away from me. Go to the eternal fire that's ready for the devil and his angels. You never did any of these things for me. You did nothing for the littlest member of my family. So you never did it to me.'"

Then Jesus told his disciples: "The Passover is in two days. Then I'll be arrested and crucified."

*Questions: Jesus said the people did good things for him. Who did they really help? What did Jesus give these people?*

82

# The Lord's Last Meal
## Luke 22:7-20; Matthew 26:26-28

The Passover had come. Peter and John prepared the feast in a house in Jerusalem. Jesus and the disciples ate together in a large upstairs room. "I've been looking forward to this Passover," he said. "I want to eat this meal with you before I suffer. I'll never eat it again until the kingdom comes."

Jesus took a loaf of bread. "Take and eat this. It represents my body which is broken for you."

Then he took a cup of wine. "Take this and share it. It represents the blood which I will shed for forgiveness of sins."

*Questions: What does the loaf of bread represent? What does the cup of wine represent?*

# The Master Washes
# His Servants Feet
### John 13:3-16

Jesus got up from the meal and poured water into a pan. He brought a towel and began to wash his disciple's feet. It came to Peter's turn. He said, "Lord, are you going to wash my feet?"

Jesus answered, "You don't understand why I'm doing this. But later you'll see."

"You'll never wash my feet!" Peter declared.

"Unless I wash your feet, you don't belong to me. You call me 'Lord' and 'Master,' and I've washed your feet. So you should do the same to each other. The servants are not greater than their master."

*Questions: Why did Jesus say he had to wash Peter's feet? Why should the disciples wash each other's feet?*

# "One of you will betray me"
### John 13:21-38

Jesus was troubled. "One of you will betray me," he said. The disciples looked at each other. They didn't know who he was talking about. Peter signaled John to ask Jesus who he was talking about.

"Lord," asked John, "who is it?"

"The one to whom I give this piece of bread." Jesus gave the bread to Judas Iscariot. Just then Satan entered into Judas. "Do what you're going to do quickly," Jesus said. No one at the table knew why he said this. Some thought that Jesus wanted Judas to buy something for the festival. Others thought it meant that Judas should give something to the poor. After he took the bread Judas quickly went out. It was nighttime.

"I'll only be with you a little longer," said Jesus. "Here is a new commandment for you. Love one another just as I've loved you. You cannot come to the place I'm going. But you'll follow afterward."

Peter said, "Lord, why can't I follow you now? I'll lay down my life for you."

"I'll tell you what you'll really do. Listen for the rooster to crow tomorrow morning. By then you'll have rejected me three times."

*Questions: What is the Lord's new commandment? What would Peter do before the rooster crowed?*

85

# In a Garden Called Gethsemane
*Matthew 26:30-46*

They sang a hymn and went to the Mount of Olives. At a garden called Gethsemane, Jesus said, "Sit here. I'll go over there and pray." With Peter, James, and John, he went to pray. "I am deeply saddened," he told them. "Stay awake with me here." And Jesus went aside alone.

He threw himself on the ground praying. "My Father, don't make me do this. But this is what you want. So I'll give up what I want."

He found the three disciples sleeping. "Get up, let's go. It is time for me to be betrayed."

*Questions: What did Jesus ask the Father when he prayed? What did the disciples do while Jesus was praying?*

# The Arrest of Jesus Christ
## Matthew 26:47-56

Judas Iscariot arrived at Gethsemane. With him was a large crowd with swords and clubs. They were sent by the leading priests. "The one I kiss is Jesus," Judas told them. "Arrest him."

Judas quickly walked to Jesus. "Hello, Teacher!" he said, and then he kissed him.

"Friend," said Jesus, "do what you came to do." Then he spoke to the crowd: "You've come to arrest me with swords and clubs. Am I a bandit? I taught you everyday in the temple. You didn't arrest me there." All the disciples ran from the garden and Jesus was led away.

*Questions: How did the crowd know who Jesus was? What name did Jesus call Judas?*

87

# A Rooster Crows, Peter Weeps
### Luke 22:54-62

They took Jesus into the high priest's house. Outside the crowd waited. Peter joined them. A girl stared at him in the firelight. "He was with Jesus," she said.

"Woman," said Peter, "I don't know him."

Later, someone else said, "You're his follower."

"Man, I am not."

Then someone insisted, "He's from Galilee. I know this man was with Jesus."

"Man," Peter cursed, "I don't know what you're talking about!"

While Peter spoke, a rooster crowed. Jesus glanced at Peter. Jesus had mentioned that Peter would deny him. Peter remembered this, walked away, and bitterly wept.

*Questions: How many times did Peter say he didn't know Jesus? What happened after Peter said he didn't know Jesus?*

# "He should die!"
### Luke 22:63-71

That night they mocked and beat and blindfolded Jesus. The next morning the leaders and chief priests gathered. Guards brought Jesus to them. They said, "If you are the Christ, tell us."

He replied, "If I tell you, you won't believe. If I ask you questions, you won't answer. But from now on I'll be seated at God's throne."

They asked, "Are you saying that you're the Son of God?"

"You say that I am," He answered.

"There!" they declared. "He said it himself. For this he should die!"

They tied Jesus up and led him away.

*Questions: Where did Jesus say he would soon be sitting? What did Jesus say that caused them to want to kill him?*

# The Death of Judas Iscariot
### Matthew 27:3-10

Judas Iscariot, the man who betrayed Jesus, heard Jesus was to die. So he changed his mind about what he'd done. He brought the thirty pieces of silver back to the priests. "I've sinned," said Judas. "Jesus is an innocent man."

"Why should that matter to us?" answered the leading priests. "What you've done is your problem."

Judas threw the coins in front of the priests in the temple. Then he ran away and hanged himself. The priests took the silver. But they said, "Moses' law says we can't put this in the offering. It is money that was used for death." They talked about this problem for a while. Then they decided to buy the potter's field with the money. It would be used to bury people who weren't Jews. This is why this field has always been called the Field of Blood.

Hundreds of years before this happened, the prophet Zechariah predicted it would. "They took the thirty pieces of silver," wrote Zechariah. "This is the price set for the servant of Israel. They gave them as the price for the potter's field. This is as the Lord commanded."

*Questions: What did Judas tell the priests about Jesus? Why wouldn't the priests give Judas' money to the temple offering?*

# "This man is innocent"
## *Luke 23:1-7; John 18:28-38*

The priests and leaders went to Pilate's palace. Pontius Pilate was the Roman ruler in Jerusalem. Jesus stood in front of Pilate as they accused him: "This man says that he, not your emperor, is our king."

"Are you the Jew's king?" Pilate asked Jesus.

"You say I'm a king. But I came for one reason: To bring the truth."

"What is truth?" scoffed Pilate. Then he told the Jews, "This man is innocent."

But they insisted. "He upsets people everywhere, from Galilee to Jerusalem."

"Herod is in charge in Galilee," said Pilate. "Take him to Herod."

*Questions: What did the priests say Jesus did wrong? What did Pilate tell them about Jesus?*

91

# "Crucify him! Crucify him!"
## *Luke 23:8-12*

Herod was happy. He'd heard of Jesus and hoped he'd do a miracle for him. This was his chance. But Jesus didn't answer any of his questions. The leading priests kept up their complaints about Jesus. Herod and his soldiers treated him shamefully and mocked him. Finally, they sent him back to Pilate. Jesus arrived wearing a royal robe. This was a joke about Jesus being king.

"This man hasn't done anything wrong," Pilate told them. "Herod doesn't seem to think so either. That's why he sent Jesus back to me. He's done nothing worth dying for. I'll just whip him and let him go." By this time many people had gathered.

"Away with him!" shouted the crowd. "Let Barabbas out of prison instead." Barabbas was a murderer. But Pilate still wanted to let Jesus go. The crowd kept shouting, "Crucify him! Crucify him!" Pilate tried one more time but they shouted him down. So Pilate let the murderer Barabbas out of prison. He then took Jesus, had him whipped, and gave him to the crowd.

Herod and Pilate had never liked each other. But the day they questioned Jesus, the two men became friends.

*Questions: Why was Herod happy to see Jesus? Why did the soldiers dress Jesus in a royal robe?*

# Crucified with Criminals
## Luke 23:26-43

They took Jesus away. The crowd made Simon of Cyrene carry Jesus' cross. Women mourned for Jesus. "Don't weep for me," he said. "Weep for yourselves. One day soon you'll cry to the mountains, 'Cover us! Our enemies have come to kill us!'"

Two criminals were led away to die with Jesus. At a place called the Skull, the men were nailed to crosses. Jesus was crucified with a criminal on each side. The soldiers played gambling games to win Jesus' clothes. The leaders scoffed at Jesus. "He saved others. If he's God's Christ he should save himself." The soldiers also mocked by offering him vinegar to drink. Even Pilate put a sign on the cross: "This is the King of the Jews."

One of the crucified criminals joined the cursing. "Are you the Christ? Save yourself and us."

"Don't you fear God?" said the other. "We deserve to be crucified. But this man's done no wrong." Then he said, "Jesus, remember me when you come into your kingdom."

"I'll tell you the truth," answered Jesus, hanging from his cross. "Today you'll be with me in Paradise."

*Questions: What did the leaders say Jesus should do? What did the believing criminal ask Jesus to do for him?*

# The Death of Jesus Christ
### Matthew 27:45-54; John 19:30

Darkness fell as Jesus hung on the cross. Darkness continued from noon to three that afternoon. Then Jesus loudly cried, "My God, my God, why have you abandoned me?" People watching thought he called Elijah. Then he said, "It is finished," and stopped breathing. At that moment, the curtain in the temple was torn. It ripped from top to bottom. This opened the holy of holies. An earthquake rumbled across the land and the rocks were split.

The captain of the Roman guards saw these things and was terrified. "Absolutely, this man was God's Son," he declared.

*Questions: What happened when Jesus stopped breathing? What did the Roman captain say about Jesus?*

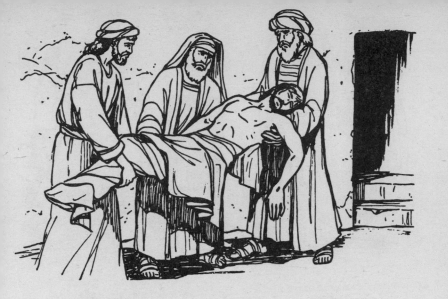

# A New Tomb in the Rock
### Matthew 27:57-66; John 19:38-42

That evening Joseph from Arimathea took Jesus' body from the cross. Together with Nicodemus, he wrapped the body in spices and clean linen. They laid it in a new tomb Joseph had cut in the rock. A heavy rock was rolled across the tomb's door. They left the garden.

The leading priests and Pharisees went to Pilate. "That liar, Jesus, said he'd come back from death," they said. "Send soldiers to guard the tomb for three days. Then his disciples can't steal the body." So they sealed the tomb shut and set guards over it.

*Questions: Who was the man who helped Joseph bury Jesus? Why did the priests put guards at Jesus' tomb?*

# "He's left death behind"
## Matthew 28:1-7

The sun was rising Sunday morning, the third day since Jesus' death. Mary from Bethany and Mary Magdalene came to his tomb. Suddenly, an earthquake rumbled. An angel had rolled away the stone. He sat by the open tomb flashing like lightening. The guards fell down, stunned with fear.

The angel spoke: "Don't be afraid, women. I know you're looking for Jesus. He isn't here. He's left death behind, just as he said he would. Here, look where he lay. Quickly, go tell his disciples this: Jesus is waiting for them in Galilee. Meet him there."

*Questions: What happened when the angel moved the stone away from Jesus' tomb? Where did the angel say Jesus was waiting?*

# "I've seen the Lord!"
## *John 20:1-18*

Mary Magdalene stood alone weeping by the tomb. She turned around. There was Jesus! But Mary thought he was the gardener. "Sir," she said, "have you taken away my Lord? Tell me where you've laid him."

Jesus said to her, "Mary."

"Teacher!"

"Don't hold onto me," he said. "I haven't yet gone up to my Father. Go, tell my brothers this: I'm going up to my Father and your Father. I'm going to my God and your God."

Mary Magdalene went and announced to the disciples, "I've seen the Lord!" She told them what had happened.

*Questions: What did Mary think had happened to Jesus? Where did Jesus say he was going?*

# Jesus Walks to Emmaus
## Luke 24:13-27

That day two disciples traveled from Jerusalem to Emmaus. They talked together about the things that had happened. A man began walking with them. They didn't recognize Jesus. "What are you talking about?" Jesus asked them.

"Haven't you heard about Jesus? He was a mighty prophet who was just crucified. But angels told some women he's now alive. Then his tomb was found empty."

"Don't you know that this had to happen to Christ?" Jesus explained the writings of Moses and the prophets to them. He showed them what the Scriptures said about Christ.

*Questions: Who walked with the two disciples to Emmaus? What did Jesus explain to the two disciples?*

# Jesus Appears in Jerusalem
## Luke 24:28-37

The two disciples didn't recognize Jesus. In Emmaus they sat down to eat together. Jesus took the bread, blessed and broke it. When he gave it to them they saw who he was. But Jesus had vanished.

They rushed back to Jerusalem and told the disciples: "Our hearts were burning within when he spoke to us on the road."

And they were told: "Jesus has appeared to Peter, too!" Just then they were startled and terrified. Jesus himself stood among them.

"Peace be with you," he said. But they thought they were seeing a ghost.

*Questions: What did Jesus do that helped the two disciples know him? What did Jesus say to the disciples when he stood among them?*

# Jesus Appears in Jerusalem
### Part Two
### Luke 24:38-49; John 20:24-28

Returning from death, Jesus stood with his disciples in Jerusalem. "Why is there doubt and fear in your hearts? Touch me and see." The disciples were so happy, but couldn't believe their eyes. "Have you anything to eat?" asked Jesus. They watched while Jesus ate.

As he opened their spiritual understanding, they heard what Moses and the prophets had written about him. "Christ will suffer and rise from the dead, and the whole world will know it," said Jesus. You've seen and understood all this.

"Soon I'll send you the Holy Spirit as my Father promised. Stay here in the city until power from above covers you like clothing."

The disciple named Thomas, didn't see these things. He didn't believe it had happened. "I'll have to touch his wounds before I believe," he said. A week later, the doors were shut. Suddenly Jesus stood among them.

"Reach out, Thomas," he said. "Touch my hands. Don't doubt, believe."

"My Lord and my God," answered Thomas as he touched Jesus.

*Questions: What did Jesus do to prove that he wasn't a ghost? What did Thomas say when he touched Jesus?*

# Jesus Serves Breakfast
# on the Seashore
### John 21:1-12

Seven of Jesus' disciples, including Peter agreed to go fishing in the Sea of Tiberias. Fishing all night, they caught nothing.

At daybreak, Jesus stood on the beach. The disciples didn't know it was Jesus.

"Children," he called, "you have no fish, do you?"

"No," they replied.

"Cast your net on the right side of the boat. There you'll find some." So the disciples cast the net. They weren't able to haul it into the boat. It was full to bursting with fish.

John exclaimed to Peter, "It's the Lord!" When Peter heard this he jumped overboard into the sea. The other disciples rowed ashore dragging the net full of fish. They weren't far from shore so Peter swam to the beach. There they found a fire with fish and bread cooking on it.

"Bring some more fish," said Jesus. They dragged the net ashore. It was full of 153 big fish, but the net wasn't torn. "Come and have breakfast," invited Jesus.

*Questions: How did the disciples know where to catch fish? What did Jesus offer the disciples when they came ashore?*

101

# "Do you love me?"
## John 21:12-25

As they stood by the fire, no disciple dared ask, "Who are you?" They knew it was the Lord. Jesus took the bread and gave it to them. He did the same with the fish.

When they finished breakfast Jesus spoke to Peter: "Peter, do you love me more than these fish?"

"Yes, Lord. You know that I love you."

"Then feed my lambs," Jesus replied. Then he asked Peter the same question a second time. "Do you love me?"

"Yes, Lord. You know that I love you."

"Then tend my sheep." Then for a third time Jesus asked, "Do you love me?" Peter felt hurt that Jesus had to ask this so many times.

"Lord," he answered, "you know everything. You know that I love you."

Jesus said, "Feed my sheep. I'll tell you the truth, Peter. When you were young, you did whatever you wished. But when you're old it will be different. Someone else will take you where you don't want to go." This meant that Peter would someday die because he served God.

Jesus did so many things. The world can't hold all the books that could be written about him.

*Questions: How many times did Jesus ask, "Do you love me?" Why did Peter feel hurt?*

# Jesus is Taken Into Heaven
## Acts 1:3-11

Jesus Christ proved that he was alive many times. For forty days he stayed with the disciples speaking about God's kingdom. He ordered them not to leave Jerusalem. Rather they were to wait there for the Father's promise. "I mentioned this to you before," he said. "John baptized with water. But in a few days, you'll be baptized with the Holy Spirit."

"Lord," they asked, "Is now the time you'll bring the kingdom to Israel?" They were gathered together on the Mount of Olives.

"You can't know the times the Father has set for these things. But you will receive power. The Holy Spirit will come upon you like clothing. Then you'll speak for me starting in Jerusalem. Then in Judea, Samaria, and to the ends of the earth."

After Jesus said this, he was lifted up as they watched. Then a cloud took him out of sight. While he was going, the disciples gazed toward heaven. Two men wearing white clothes stood with them. "Men from Galilee, why are you standing there looking up? This Jesus has been taken from you into heaven. But he'll come back in the same way as you saw him go."

*Questions: With what would the disciples be baptized? How will Jesus come back?*

# Pentecost in Jerusalem
### Part One
### Acts 2:1-11

The disciples constantly prayed together after Jesus went away in the cloud.

Fifty days after Jesus was crucified, there was a big holiday. It was called Pentecost. At that time, many thousands of people visited Jerusalem. The disciples were all together that day. Suddenly, a sound like violent wind filled the house. Fire appeared and rested on each of them. They were all filled with the Holy Spirit. The Spirit made them able to speak in other languages. Then a curious crowd gathered. They were from many different nations. But they each heard the gospel in their own language.

*Questions: What was the name of the holiday in Jerusalem? What ability did the Holy Spirit give to the disciples?*

104

# Pentecost in Jerusalem
*Part Two*
*Acts 2:12-39*

Everyone was amazed and puzzled. They each heard their own language! "What does this mean?" some asked. Others sneered, "They're drunk on new wine."

Then Peter stood up. "People from Judea and all who live in Jerusalem. We're not drunk. It's only nine in the morning. Long ago the prophet Joel wrote: 'In the last days I'll pour my Spirit on everyone. Then, those who call on the Lord's name will be saved.'

"Jesus of Nazareth did miracles among you, but in God's plan, you killed him. This same Jesus, God brought back from death. We have seen him. He's now at God's right hand. The Father has given Jesus the promise of the Holy Spirit.

Peter's words cut them to the heart. They asked, "What shall we do?"

"Everyone, turn from your sins, be forgiven, and be baptized in the name of Jesus Christ. You'll be given the Holy Spirit as a gift. This promise is for you, your children, and all who are far away." Three thousand people believed in Jesus that day.

*Questions: What happens to those who call on the name of the Lord? What is the gift people get when they believe in Jesus?*

105

# Walking and Leaping
# and Praising God
### Acts 3:1-8

"Give me money please," begged a disabled man near the temple. "I've been crippled since I was born." Peter and John, passing nearby, heard the man's plea.

"I have no silver or gold," Peter said to him. "But I'll give you what I have. In the name of Jesus Christ of Nazareth, stand up and walk." Peter took the man's hand and helped him up. Instantly, the man's feet and ankles became strong. Jumping up, he walked. The man went into the temple with Peter and John. He was walking and leaping and praising God.

*Questions: What name did Peter use to heal the man? What three things did the man do when he went into the temple?*

# Arrested in the Temple
### Acts 3:9-4:4

"People of Israel," Peter spoke in the temple. "Why are you amazed and wondering about this man? He wasn't healed because we are powerful or holy. This is the way your ancestor's God has glorified his Son, Jesus. Pilate wanted to free Jesus, but you wanted the murderer Barabbas instead. And so you killed the source of life. But God brought him back from death. We have seen him. Faith in the name of Jesus Christ has made this man strong.

"I know that you didn't know what you were doing. You ignorantly killed Jesus. The prophets all said this would happen to Christ. But now, turn to God so your sins will be wiped out. Then refreshing times will come because of the Lord. In time, God will send Jesus, your Christ, back again."

Peter and John were speaking to the people. The priests and the temple captain came to them. These men were annoyed that the disciples were teaching in the temple. Especially that they said, "In Jesus there is return from death." So they arrested Peter and John. They were held until the next day. But 5,000 people believed in Jesus that day.

*Questions: What made the disabled man strong? What did Peter and John say that annoyed the priests?*

# The Companions of Jesus
### Acts 4:5-21

The next day Peter and John stood in front of the high priest and other leaders. "In whose name did you do this work?" they were asked.

Peter was filled with the Holy Spirit. "Leaders of the people," he said. Do you want to know why this man is standing here in good health? It is by the name of Jesus Christ of Nazareth—the man you crucified, and God brought back from death. Salvation is only found in him. No other name has been given by which we must be saved."

The leaders saw Peter and John's boldness. They saw that they were common, uneducated men. Also, they knew Peter and John were companions of Jesus. The priests and leaders were amazed.

"What should we do with them?" they asked each other. "Everyone in Jerusalem has heard of this miracle. We can't say it didn't happen." So they ordered the disciples, "Never speak again in the name of Jesus."

"We can't keep from speaking of what we've seen and heard," they answered. And the people praised God for what had happened.

*Questions: What did Peter say was special about Jesus' name? Peter and John were common men and not educated. What was special about them?*

# "You lied to God!"
## Acts 4:32-5:11

With great power and in one accord, the apostles declared the Lord's resurrection. Great grace was upon them all. Those who owned houses sold them. The money was given to those who where in need.

But a man named Ananias sold some property. His wife, Sapphira, agreed that they keep some of the money. Only part of it was given for the poor.

"Ananias," said Peter, "why has Satan caused you to lie? The Holy Spirit knows you held back part of the money. When you sold the land, the money was yours. Now, you have lied to God!"

Hearing this, Ananias fell down and died. Young men took the body out for burial. Later, Ananias' wife came in. She didn't know what had happened. "Did you and your husband sell your land?" asked Peter.

"Yes," Sapphira answered.

"Why did you test the Lord's Spirit? There are the men who buried your husband. They're ready to carry you out." Immediately, she fell to the floor, dead. Sapphira was buried beside her husband. And the fear of God came over the whole church.

*Questions: Why were none of the believers needy? Why did Ananias die?*

109

# Arrested in the Temple Again
### Acts 5:14-26

Great numbers of men and women believed. The sick were even carried out into the streets of Jerusalem. They simply wanted Peter's shadow to fall on them as he passed by. People brought the sick in from the towns around. They all were cured.

Then the high priest took action. He and the other priests and teachers were jealous. So they arrested the apostles and put them into prison. But during the night an angel opened the prison doors. "Go," said the angel. "Stand in the temple and tell the people about this life." So at dawn, the apostles were in the temple again. There they went on with their teaching.

That day the priests called for the prisoners to be brought. But the police didn't find the apostles in the prison. "We found the prison locked," they reported. "The guards were standing at the doors. But no one was inside." Everyone was puzzled.

Then another report came: "The men you put in prison are teaching in the temple!" The temple police quietly brought the apostles to the high priest. They were afraid of being stoned by the people.

*Questions: Why did the priests arrest the apostles? What did the apostles do when they were released from prison?*

# Fighting Against God
### Acts 5:27-42

The apostles stood in the council. "We gave you strict orders!" said the high priest. "Don't teach in this name again. Yet you've filled Jerusalem with your teaching."

Then Peter spoke for all the apostles: "We must obey God instead of any human power. You hanged Jesus on a cross and there he died. But God brought him back from death. Now Jesus is by God's side as the Leader and Savior. He wants to give Israel forgiveness of sins. We simply speak of what we've seen."

The council was enraged and wanted to kill the apostles. But a wise teacher named Gamaliel spoke up. "Fellow Israelites, think carefully about this matter. I say, let them alone. If their work is merely human, it will fail. But if it comes from God, you can't stop them. In fact, you may be found fighting against God." The council was won over by Gamaliel's reasoning.

The apostles were whipped and ordered not to speak in Jesus' name. They were released rejoicing: "We are worthy to suffer for his name!" And they didn't stop declaring and teaching, "Jesus is the Christ."

*Questions: Where did Peter say Jesus is today? What did the wise teacher Gamaliel say to do about the disciples?*

# A Man Full of Faith
## Acts 6:1-15

God's word kept on spreading in Jerusalem. The number of disciples grew larger. Even a great many priests came to faith in Christ.

Seven men were chosen from among the believers. They were full of the Holy Spirit and wisdom. Their job was to care for the sharing of food among the believers. One of these was Stephen; a man full of faith, grace, and power. He did great wonders and signs among the people. Some among the Jews rose up and argued with Stephen. But they couldn't stand against his wisdom and spirit. So they secretly paid people to accuse him: "We've heard Stephen say terrible things against Moses and God." The people, leaders, and teachers of Moses' law were all angry.

Stephen was forced to go to in the council of rulers. There people lied about him. "He says Jesus of Nazareth will destroy the temple," they said. "He wants to change the traditions that Moses gave us."

The high priest looked at Stephen. "Are these things true?" he asked. The whole council also looked deeply into Stephen's face. They saw that it was like the face of an angel.

*Questions: What kind of a man was Stephen? What were the lies that were told about Stephen?*

# Stephen is Stoned to Death
### Acts 7:2-60

Stephen gave the council a meaningful speech. Beginning from Abraham, he traced the history of the Jewish people. But the council became enraged. "Your ancestors persecuted every prophet," Stephen said. "These prophets predicted that Christ would come. And now you're his murderers." With a shout they rushed him. "Look," Stephen said, "the heavens are opened. There's Jesus standing next to God." They covered their ears and dragged him from Jerusalem. There Stephen was stoned to death. "Lord Jesus, receive my spirit," he prayed. Then he knelt saying, "Don't hold this sin against them." And Stephen died.

*Questions: What did Stephen see in heaven? What did he pray about the people who stoned him to death?*

# Saul—The Persecutor of Jesus
## Acts 9:1-5

A young man named Saul approved of Stephen's death. Then Saul began to run the believers out of Jerusalem. He breathed threats and murder against the disciples. Dragged from their houses, believers were jailed.

Saul went to the high priest for permission to go to Damascus. He planned to arrest men and women who followed Jesus' way. When Saul came near Damascus a light from heaven flashed around him. He fell to the ground. A voice said, "Saul, Saul, why do you persecute me?"

"Who are you, Lord?" asked Saul.

"I'm Jesus, the one you're harassing."

*Questions: Why did Saul go to Damascus? What did Jesus ask Saul?*

114

# Saul—The Believer in Jesus
## Acts 9:6-19

Saul lay on the ground blinded by a light from heaven. Jesus himself spoke: "Get up and go into the city. There you'll be told what to do." The men traveling with Saul were standing speechless. They heard the voice but saw no one. They led Saul by the hand into Damascus. For three days, Saul was blind and ate nothing.

Then the Lord spoke to a disciple named Ananias. "A man from Tarsus named Saul has seen a vision. In it you, Ananias, touch him so he can see again. Go and do this."

"Lord," Ananias said, "I've heard of this man. He's done so much evil to your saints in Jerusalem. He's come here to arrest people who call on your name."

"Go, Ananias. I've chosen Saul to bring my name to people of all nations. He'll bring my name to kings and the people of Israel. I will personally teach him how much he must suffer. This suffering will be for my name."

Ananias went. "Brother Saul," he said, "the Lord Jesus has sent me. Receive your sight. Be filled with the Holy Spirit." Instantly, Saul could see again. He was baptized, ate a meal, and got his strength back.

*Questions: Who did Ananias say Saul was going to arrest? For what would Saul suffer?*

# Saul—The Preacher of Jesus
## Acts 9:20-31

Saul stayed for several days with the disciples in Damascus. Immediately, he went to the Jewish synagogues. "Jesus is the Son of God," he declared.

"Isn't this the man who made havoc in the church in Jerusalem?" After awhile some people plotted to kill Saul. But Saul found out. The gates were watched day and night. So the disciples brought him to a hole in the city's wall. They lowered Saul down in a basket and he escaped.

Saul returned to Jerusalem. He tried to join the disciples there. But they were afraid. "He doesn't believe in Jesus," they said. But a disciple named Barnabas introduced Saul to the apostles. Barnabas told them how Saul had seen the Lord.

"The Lord spoke to him in Damascus," said Barnabas. "And Saul boldly preached the gospel there." So Saul stayed with the church in Jerusalem. He spoke and argued with the Greek Jews. But they plotted to kill him. So the believers put Saul on a boat in Caesarea. From there, he sailed home to Tarsus.

And the whole church had peace and was built up.

*Questions: What did Saul tell the people in the synagogues of Damascus? How did Saul escape from Damascus?*

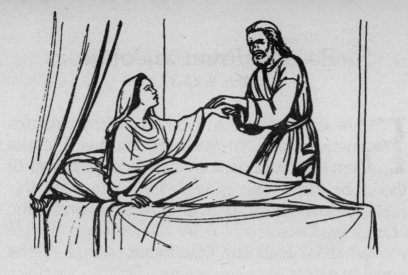

# "Tabitha is alive!"
## Acts 9:36-43

Peter went here and there among all the believers. In Joppa was a disciple named Tabitha. She was faithful to do good works and help others. But she grew sick and died. Two men were sent to Peter. "Please come with us quickly," they asked.

At Tabitha's house, the widows were weeping. Peter sent them out, knelt down, and prayed. Then he said, "Tabitha, get up." She opened her eyes and sat up. The news went out: "Tabitha is alive!" Many believed in the Lord.

Peter stayed in Joppa for some time in Simon the tanner's house.

*Questions: What did Peter do when he went into Tabitha's house? What happened in Joppa after people heard what had happened to Tabitha?*

# Peter's Vision in Joppa
## Acts 10:1-23

In Caesarea lived a Roman soldier named Cornelius. So Cornelius wasn't a Jew. He was a Gentile. Yet he was true to God and gave to the poor. He always prayed. One afternoon this man had a vision. An angel came and said, "Cornelius?"

"What is it, Lord?" Cornelius stared at the angel in terror.

"Send men to Joppa and find Peter at Simon's house." Quickly, Cornelius sent for Peter.

About noon the next day Peter went to Simon's roof to pray. While he waited, Peter fell into a trance. He saw a large sheet coming from heaven. In it were all kinds of animals. A voice spoke, "Peter get up and eat these animals." But the animals in the sheet were banned by Jewish law. So, to Peter, the meat wasn't clean.

"No, Lord," said Peter. "I've never eaten any unclean meat."

"God has made this meat clean. Don't call it unclean again." Peter was puzzled about this. Just then the men came from Cornelius. The next day, Peter went with them to Cornelius's house in Caesarea.

*Questions: Cornelius was true to God. So what two things did he do? Why didn't Peter want to eat the animals in the sheet?*

# The Spirit and the Gentiles
## Acts 10:24-48

Cornelius' relatives and close friends were all gathered. Finally, Peter arrived. Cornelius fell at Peter's feet to worship him. "Get up," said Peter, "I'm only a mortal man."

In the house, Peter said, "You know that I'm a Jew. It's against our law to visit a Gentile. But God told me not to call anyone unclean." This was the meaning of Peter's vision two days before. "So I had no problem coming here. What do you want?"

Cornelius replied, "Four days ago a man in dazzling clothes came to me. 'Cornelius,' he said, 'God has heard your prayers. Send to Joppa and find Peter.' I did this and you're kind enough to come. We're here in the presence of God to listen to you."

So Peter began to tell them the good news about Jesus Christ. He mentioned forgiveness of sins in Jesus' name but had to stop. The Holy Spirit had fallen on everyone listening. The Jewish believers with Peter were astounded. The Father's gift of the Holy Spirit had been poured on the Gentiles! "Let's baptize these people in the name of Jesus Christ," said Peter. And they stayed there for several days.

*Questions: Why did Peter have no problem being with Gentiles? Why were the Jewish believers astounded?*

# The Lord Rescues Peter
### Acts 12:1-11

King Herod laid his violent hands on some of the believers. He had James, John's brother, killed. Then Peter was arrested. The church urgently prayed to God.

Peter slept, chained to two soldiers. An angel entered the prison, "Get up quickly. Put on your sandals." Peter did so. "Follow me." The apostle thought he was seeing a vision. They passed through the guards. By itself the prison gate swung open. They walked along a city lane. The angel suddenly disappeared.

"The Lord has rescued me," realized Peter. "The people will not see me die."

*Questions: Who did Herod have killed? What did the church do when Peter was arrested?*

# Peter and the Prayer Meeting
## Acts 12:12-23

Peter realized he was saved from death. At once he went to Mary's house where the church was praying. Mary was Mark's mother.

Rhoda, Mary's maid, heard a knock on the gate. When she answered, Rhoda recognized Peter's voice. She was overjoyed. Instead of opening the gate, she ran to tell the others. "You're out of your mind," they said. But Rhoda insisted. They then said, "It's Peter's angel."

Meanwhile Peter continued knocking. They opened the gate and were amazed. "Quiet, quiet," Peter whispered. He described what had happened to him. "Tell this to the Lord's brother, James, and to the believers," he said. Peter then went to another place.

In those days, Herod feuded with the people of Tyre. They came to him to make peace. They had no choice since King Herod controlled their food. Herod put on his royal robes and sat on his throne. He gave a vain speech to the people. "It's the voice of a god," they shouted. "Herod is more than a man!"

Instantly, an angel of God struck Herod down. He hadn't given God the glory. Herod, eaten up inside by worms, died.

*Questions: Who did the church think Peter was? Why did the angel strike Herod down?*

# The Believers Are Called Christians

### Acts 11:19-30

When Stephen was killed, believers scattered all over the Middle East. In Antioch some told the Greeks the good news of Jesus. A great number of Gentiles became believers and turned to the Lord.

The church in Jerusalem heard of this. They sent Barnabas to Antioch. There he saw God's grace among the people. Barnabas rejoiced. "Be faithful to the Lord," he told them. "Stay devoted to him." Barnabas was a good man; full of the Holy Spirit and faith. A great many people were brought to the Lord.

Then Barnabas went to Tarsus to look for Saul. He found him and brought him back to Antioch. For an entire year, they met with the church. Barnabas and Saul taught many, many people. The believers there were not at all like Jews. And they'd changed in ways that made them unlike Gentiles. So it was in Antioch that believers were first called "Christians."

At that time a famine came. Believers in Judea suffered without food. So the church in Antioch sent Barnabas and Saul. They brought aid to the churches in Judea.

*Questions: What did Barnabas tell the new Gentile believers in Antioch? Where were believers first called "Christians?"*

# The Apostles Are Sent Out
### Acts 13:1-12

Now in the church at Antioch there were prophets and teachers. They prayed together worshiping God. The Holy Spirit said to them, "Set aside Barnabas and Saul. I've called them for my work." The leaders of the church prayed and laid their hands on them. The Holy Spirit sent Barnabas and Saul out. They took Mark and set off. The three apostles sailed to the island of Cyprus. There they spoke God's word in the Jewish synagogues.

They traveled through the whole island. At Paphos lived a magician, a false-prophet named Bar-Jesus. The ruler of Cyprus, Sergius Paulus, wanted to hear God's word. But the magician tried to turn him away from the faith. Saul, now called Paul, watched him carefully. Paul was filled with the Holy Spirit. "You son of the devil," He said. "You enemy of all that's right. Stop making the Lord's straight paths crooked. God's hand is against you. You'll not be able to see for awhile."

Shortly, the magician could only see darkness. He had to have someone lead him by the hand. Sergius Paulus saw this and believed. He was delighted at the teaching about the Lord.

*Questions: Who sent Barnabas and Saul out of Antioch? What is Saul's new name?*

# A Light for the Gentiles
### Acts 13:13-52

Paul and his companions sailed away from Paphos. They reached the mainland at Pamphilia. There, Mark left them and returned to Jerusalem. The apostles traveled inland to another city named Antioch. This was in Pisidia. On the sabbath Paul spoke to the Jews in their synagogue. He traced the history of the Jewish people. This history ended with the death of Jesus. Paul told his listeners that Jesus had returned from death.

Almost the whole city gathered the next sabbath. The Jews saw the crowds and became jealous. They denied that Paul spoke the truth. But Paul and Barnabas were bold. "God wanted his word to come to you first. But you don't seem to think you're worthy of eternal life. So we're going to tell the Gentiles. God has commanded this. He said, 'You're to be a light for the Gentiles. Then you can bring my salvation to the ends of the earth.'"

When the Gentiles heard this, they were glad. They praised the word of the Lord. The Lord's word spread all over the area. But the Jews drove Paul and Barnabas away. So they left, glad to shake Antioch's dust from their feet.

*Questions: What did the jealous Jews say about Paul? Why were the Gentiles in Antioch glad?*

# "The gods have come to us!"
## Acts 14:1-26

Paul and Barnabas, were almost stoned like Stephen in Antioch. But they escaped to Lystra in Lycaonia.

Looking at a crippled man, Paul exclaimed, "Stand up on your feet." And the man jumped up and began to walk. The crowds saw this.

"The gods have come down to us as men!" they exclaimed. "This one," they shouted pointing at Barnabas, "is Zeus. The other man does all the talking. That means he's Hermes!" This was Paul. The priest of the temple of Zeus brought oxen for sacrifices.

Paul and Barnabas rushed into the crowd. "Friends!" they shouted. "Why are you doing this? We're human just like you. We've brought good news: Turn from these worthless things! The living God made heaven and earth and everything in them. He fills your bellies with food and your hearts with joy!" They were barely able to stop the sacrifices.

Then people came from Antioch and excited the crowd against Paul. He was stoned and dragged alive out of Lystra. Soon the apostles returned to the church at Antioch in Syria.

*Questions: What did the crowds think when Paul healed the man in Lystra? What did the apostles tell the crowds about the living God?*

125

# "We're saved through grace"
## Acts 14:27-15:1-21

The Antioch church rejoiced. God had opened the door of faith for the Gentiles! But then some people came to Antioch from Judea. They said, "You Gentile Christians must keep Moses' law."

But Paul and Barnabus said, "God is happy that the Gentiles have believed in Jesus. They don't have to do anything else to be saved." So the apostles and leaders called a meeting in Jerusalem. Paul and Barnabas went there to discuss this important problem.

The first person to speak was Peter. "Brothers, God gave the Gentiles the Holy Spirit. I was at Cornelius' house when it happened. So God must not see a difference between them and us. Anyway, no one has ever been able to keep Moses' law. We're saved through the grace of the Lord Jesus. So are the Gentiles."

Paul and Barnabas then told of the wonders God did among the Gentiles. James had the final word: "God wants to make the Gentiles into a people for his name. Let's not trouble those who are turning to God."

*Questions: What did the people from Judea say the Gentiles had to do? How did Peter say people are saved?*

126

# Across the Sea to Europe
## Acts 16:1-15

Then, Paul and Silas visited the places Paul had been before and strengthened the churches. The believers learned about the decision made in Jerusalem: They didn't have to keep the Jewish law. In Lystra Paul met Timothy. This young disciple began to travel with Paul.

They traveled due west through Asia. The Holy Spirit didn't let Paul speak God's word there. At the coast of the Aegean Sea, the travelers stopped. This was the city of Troas. Here Paul met Luke, whom he called "the beloved physician."

That night Paul had a vision of a man from Macedonia. Macedonia was a country across the Aegean Sea. The man begged, "Come help us!" Paul knew what this meant. God wanted him to leave Asia and cross the sea to Europe. There he would preach the good news.

Timothy, Luke, Silas, and Paul set sail. Two days later they landed in Philippi, the main city in Macedonia. On the sabbath they went to the riverside. Speaking to the women who prayed there, they met Lydia. Her business was selling purple cloth. Soon, Lydia and her household were baptized. The apostles stayed in Lydia's house.

*Questions: Why didn't Paul speak God's word in Asia? Who was Luke?*

127

# Paul and the Fortune-teller
### Acts 16:16-28

Luke recorded the history of Paul's travels. He wrote the following story:

In Philippi we met a slave girl who was controlled by a spirit. This spirit made her a fortune-teller. The girl's owners made money from her fortune-telling. She followed Paul around crying, "These men serve the Most High God." She did this for many days. Finally, Paul was annoyed. He spoke to the spirit. "I order you in the name of Jesus Christ. Come out of her." And it did.

The slave girl's owners couldn't make money anymore from her fortune-telling. Angry, they forced Paul and Silas to the rulers at the marketplace. "These men are disturbing our city," they said. "They want us to break the Roman law." Paul and Silas were beaten and locked in the deepest prison cell.

At midnight Paul and Silas were praying and singing hymns. Other prisoners listened to them. Suddenly, a violent earthquake shook the prison. The doors opened and the prisoners' chains fell off. The jailer awoke, saw the prison open, and grabbed his sword. He was about to kill himself. He thought his prisoners had escaped. But Paul shouted, "Don't hurt yourself! We're all here."

*Questions: Why were the slave girl's owners angry at Paul? What did Paul and Silas do in prison?*

# Paul, Silas, and the Jailer
### Acts 16:29-40

Luke's story continues:
    The jailer rushed into the prison. He fell down trembling in front of Paul and Silas. "What do I have to do to be saved?"

"Believe in the Lord Jesus and you'll be saved with your household." They spoke the Lord's word to him and his family. Next the jailer washed their wounds. Then he and his family were baptized. They sat down to a meal together rejoicing. The jailer had become a believer in God!

Returning to Lydia's home, they encouraged the brothers and sisters. Then we left Philippi.

*Questions: The jailer wanted to know how to be saved. What is the answer? What did the jailer do for Paul and Silas?*

# Harassed by Jealousy
### Acts 17:1-15

In Thessalonica, Paul went into the synagogue to discuss the Scriptures. For three sabbaths he explained why Christ had to die. He proved that Christ had to come back from death. "The Christ is Jesus," said Paul. "He's the man I'm telling you about."

Some Jews, many Greeks, and important women joined Paul and Silas. Certain Jews formed a mob with ruffians from the marketplace. The city was in an uproar. People shouted, "These people have been turning the world upside down. Now they've come to our city!"

At the nearby town of Berea, Paul entered the synagogue. These Jews were more civil than those in Thessalonica. They welcomed Paul's message eagerly. "Are these things true?" they wondered. So they studied the Scriptures everyday. Many of them believed as did some Greek women and noblemen.

But people from Thessalonica arrived. Crowds were stirred up and Paul had to flee to the coast. Timothy and Silas stayed behind while Paul traveled to Athens. There he waited for his companions.

*Questions: What happened to Paul at Thessalonica? What did the people in Berea do to understand Paul's message?*

# The Babbler Speaks of God
*Acts 17:16-25*

Paul became known in Athens as a babbler. He constantly talked about Jesus Christ. Some people there did nothing but talk about new ideas. "We'd like to know what these strange notions mean," they told Paul.

"I found an interesting altar in your city," he began. "On it was written: To An Unknown God. I declare this God, who made the world and everything in it to be the Lord of heaven and earth. He has no need of these shrines or anything humans can give. Instead, he gives us life and breath and all things."

*Questions: Why was Paul called a babbler? Why does God have no need of anything humans can give?*

# Atop a Hill in Athens
### Acts 17:26-18:4

Atop a hill in Athens Paul declared the true God: "From one ancestor God made all the different races. He decided when and where on earth they would live. Why? So they would search for the Lord, reach out and find him. He is not far from each of us. For in him we live and move and have our being. Your poets have said this very thing. They wrote: 'For we too are his children.'"

Paul continued. "Since we're God's children, how can God be a stone image shaped by human imagination. Now he commands all people to change their minds. A day has been set when the world will be judged. God has selected a man to be the judge. He's brought him back from death."

Paul's audience interrupted and scoffed. "A man brought back from death?" they laughed. But some joined Paul and believed.

After this Paul left Athens and went to Corinth. There he worked with Aquila and his wife Priscilla. They were tentmakers as was Paul. Every sabbath he would try to convince Jews and Greeks about Jesus.

*Questions: Why did God make the different races on earth? What did Paul say that made his audience scoff?*

# Paul Works like a Farmer
### Acts 18:5-23

When Silas and Timothy arrived in Corinth, Paul was very busy. He was always talking about the Scriptures with the Jews. He assured them that Jesus was the Christ. They argued and snubbed him. Paul shook the dust out of his cloak into their faces. "This means I'm through with you. You must answer to God for refusing the truth. I'm not to blame. Now I'm going to pay attention to the Gentiles."

One night the Lord spoke to Paul in a vision. "Don't be afraid," he said. "Speak and don't be silent. I'm with you and no one will harm you. Many people in Corinth belong to me."

Paul worked like a farmer among the people of Corinth. He planted the seeds of God's gospel for eighteen months. During that time, Paul wrote two letters to the believers in Thessalonica. He wanted them to live a holy, hard-working life. "Look forward to the day Jesus comes again," he wrote.

Priscilla, Aquila, and Paul then sailed for Syria. Priscilla and her husband stayed in a big city there called Ephesus. Paul continued his journey. After visiting Jerusalem, he arrived at Antioch and stayed there some time.

*Questions: What did Paul tell the Jews in Corinth? What did Paul write to the believers in Thessalonica?*

# Everyone Heard the Lord's Word
### Acts 19:1-17

Soon Paul set off on his third long journey. From Antioch he traveled by land through his hometown of Tarsus. In time he arrived back in Ephesus. For three months Paul argued in the synagogue about God's kingdom. Finally, some people said evil things about God's way. So Paul and the believers began to meet in Tyrannus' auditorium. This went on for two years. Everyone living in Asia heard the Lord's word. The Jews heard the truth and so did the Greeks.

God did amazing miracles through Paul. If someone who was sick touched his handkerchief, they were healed. At that time there were people who pretended to heal the sick. So they tried to use the name of the Lord Jesus. Sceva's seven sons once spoke to an evil spirit. "I command you by the Jesus that Paul preaches," they declared.

"I know Jesus," said the spirit. "I know Paul, too. But who are you?" And the man with the evil spirit leaped on them. He beat them badly. The seven men ran from the house naked and bleeding. Everyone in Ephesus heard of this. They were awestruck and the name of Jesus was praised.

*Questions: Why did Paul begin to meet in Tyrannus' auditorium? What did the evil spirit say to Sceva's seven sons?*

# Confusion in Ephesus
### Part One
### Acts 19:18-31

Some magicians in Ephesus became believers and burned their magic books in public. So the Lord's word grew mightily and remained.

Then a huge commotion broke out. The temple of an idol named Diana was big business in Ephesus. A silversmith named Demetrius made and sold little shrines for this goddess. He called together all the workers in his trade. "We get all our money from this business," he said. "But Paul says that hand-made gods aren't gods! Large groups of people have believed him. Our business may be ruined. Also the temple of the great goddess Diana will be scorned. Her majesty, the praise of all Asia, will be destroyed."

This news enraged the silversmiths. "Great is Diana of the Ephesians!" they shouted. The city was filled with confusion. Everyone rushed together to the city's theater. Gaius and Aristarchus, Paul's friends, were dragged with them. Paul wanted to go into the crowd. Of course his disciples wouldn't let him do this. Some of Asia's rulers were Paul's friends. They warned, "Don't go into the theater!"

*Questions: Why did Demetrius call together the other silversmiths? What did Paul say about gods that are made by hand?*

# Confusion in Ephesus
## Part Two
### Acts 19:32-20:1

The outdoor theater in Ephesus filled up with noisy people shouting various things. A man named Alexander finally quieted the crowd. But when they found out he was a Jew they shouted him down. "He doesn't worship Diana!" For two hours everyone shouted "Great is Diana of the Ephesians!"

Then the town clerk got control. "Citizens of Ephesus!" he shouted. "Everyone knows that Ephesus keeps the temple of Diana. Her statue, which fell down to us from heaven, is here. No one can say this isn't true. So you should be quiet. Don't become violent. These men haven't robbed the temple. Nor have they cursed the goddess. Demetrius, you and the silversmiths should go to court. Take your problems there to be solved. There is no reason for this! The Romans are about to accuse the whole city of rioting. So everyone go home." And that was the end of it.

After the uproar was over Paul gathered the Ephesian believers. He'd been there three years. After encouraging them, he said farewell and left for Macedonia.

*Questions: Why wouldn't the Ephesians listen to Alexander? What did Paul do before he left for Macedonia?*

136

# Paul Talked, Eutychus Slept
### Acts 20:6-17

Paul cared for the believers in Macedonia. Then he stayed three months in Greece. Setting sail for Syria, he learned of a plot against his life. So he traveled by land back through Macedonia. After several months, Paul and his companions arrived in Troas.

On Sunday they met to break bread. Since Paul was leaving the next day, he talked on until midnight. Many lamps lit the upstairs meeting room.

As Paul talked still longer, a young man named Eutychus slept. He was sitting in an open window. Suddenly, Eutychus crashed to the ground three floors below. Someone picked him up dead. Paul went down, picked him up, and said, "Don't weep. His life is still in him."

Then Paul went upstairs. He broke bread, ate, and continued to talk. This went on until dawn. Meanwhile they took Eutychus away alive. Everyone was very comforted.

Paul then sailed down the coast of Asia. "Let's be in Jerusalem by Pentecost," he said. While in the port of Miletus, Paul sent a message to Ephesus. Soon the Ephesian elders were hurrying to meet with the apostle.

*Questions: What happened to the man who slept in the meeing hall window? When did Paul want to be in Jerusalem?*

137

# Paul's Farewell
### Acts 20:18-38

The leaders of the church in Ephesus came to Miletus. "You know how I live my life," Paul began. "I humbly serve the Lord with tears. I suffer the plots against my life. If there's any way to help, I do it. I brought God's message to your city and your houses. I told everyone about turning to God and faith in Jesus.

"And now the Spirit is leading me to Jerusalem. Prison and hardship are waiting for me there. But I don't prize my life for my own sake. I just want to finish my work. This is the important thing: to declare the good news of God's grace.

"Now, I know that none of you will ever see my face again. I wasn't afraid to tell you God's whole purpose. So the rest is up to you. I hand you over to God and the message of his grace.

"Remember that I never asked for money. Instead I worked with these two hands for myself and my friends. Remember the Lord's words: 'It's more blessed to give than to receive.'" They knelt together in prayer. The men from Ephesus wept. They'd never see Paul again.

*Questions: What was the most important thing to Paul? Paul reminded them of what the Lord had said. What was this?*

# On the Way to Jerusalem
### Acts 21:1-14

The apostles sailed across the eastern end of the Great Sea. Luke continues the story:

We landed at Tyre and found the believers. Through the Spirit they told Paul, "Don't go on to Jerusalem." After seven days, we were ready to leave. Everyone followed us out of the city. We knelt on the beach, prayed, and said farewell. Then we went on board the ship and they went home.

A short voyage took us to Ptolemais and then to Caesarea. There we stayed with Philip. He had served with the martyr Stephen in Jerusalem. While we were there, a man named Agabus came down from Judea. Agabus warned us in this way: taking Paul's belt, he tied himself up. "These are the Holy Spirit's words," he said. "The Jews in Jerusalem will tie up the owner of this belt. They will give him to the Gentiles." Then everyone urged Paul not to go to Jerusalem.

"What are you doing?" asked Paul. "Your weeping is breaking my heart. I'm ready to die in Jerusalem for the Lord's name."

We said nothing more except: "Let the Lord do what he wants."

*Questions: What did Agabus say would happen to Paul in Jerusalem? What did Paul say he was ready to do?*

# Paul Enters the Temple
## Acts 21:15-27

Luke continues:

We were warmly welcomed in Jerusalem. Paul visited James and the elders. He told them of God's work with the Gentiles. They praised God for this. Then James said, "Paul, there are thousands of Jewish believers here. They all love Moses' law. But they think you teach Jews to throw out the law." This wasn't true. Paul only taught all people to trust God's grace.

"These people will soon know you're here," James continued. "So please do this: Four men are going to take a vow in the temple. Go with them and pay their fees. Then everyone will know that you care for Moses' law." Paul knew the Jews could keep the law if they wanted to. And the Gentiles didn't need to keep the law. Either way, God wants people to believe in Jesus. James and the elders in Jerusalem knew this too.

So Paul and the men entered the temple. Paul didn't do this to please God. He just wanted people to stop lying about him. But there in the temple were men who had harassed Paul in Asia. They spied their old enemy. "Here's our chance to get Paul," they plotted.

*Questions: What did the Jewish believers think Paul taught? What did Paul really teach?*

# Paul is Dragged out of the Temple
## Acts 21:27-22:1

Everything went well for Paul in the temple. At least until the men from Asia found him. "Israelites, help!" they cried and grabbed Paul. "This is the man who's against Moses' law and this temple. Look! He's brought Gentiles here and made this holy place filthy!" The people rushed together and dragged Paul out of the temple.

Paul was about to be killed but Roman soldiers rescued him. Then the captain arrested Paul and chained him. "Who's this man?" asked the captain. "What's he done?" Some in the crowd shouted one thing. Some shouted another. There was such an uproar that he couldn't hear. Paul had to be carried off by the soldiers. "Away with him!" shouted the crowd.

At a safe distance from the crowd, Paul spoke to the captain. "I'm a Jew, a citizen of Tarsus. That's an important Roman city. Please let me speak to the people." The captain gave his permission.

Paul stood on the steps and signaled the crowd for silence. "Brothers and fathers," he began, "listen to what I have to say."

*Questions: What did the men from Asia say Paul had done to the temple? What did Paul call his listeners when he began to speak?*

# A Speech in the Streets
### Acts 22:2-22

The angry crowd heard their own language and stopped to listen. "I'm a Jew, born in Tarsus," Paul said. "But here in Jerusalem I learned our ancestors' law. When the time came, I fought against the Christians. The high priest and elders can tell you this.

"They sent me to Damascus to arrest Christians there. On the way, about noon, a great light from heaven flashed. I fell to the ground. A voice said, 'Saul, Saul, why are you fighting me?'

"'Who are you, Lord?' I asked.

"'I'm Jesus of Nazareth.'

"In the city a good Jewish man named Ananias met me. 'God has chosen you,' he said. 'You'll tell the world of what you've seen and heard. Now get up and be baptized calling on his name.'

"I came back here and was praying in the temple. The Lord appeared. 'Get out of this city,' he said. 'The people won't listen to you.'

"'But Lord, I agreed when they killed Stephen,' I reasoned.

"'Go, I am sending you far away to the Gentiles.'"

When they heard the word "Gentiles" the crowd erupted with violent anger.

*Questions: What story did Paul tell the crowd? Why did the crowd get angry again?*

# Saved from the Raging Crowd
### Acts 22:22-30

"Away with such a fellow from the earth!" the crowd raged. "He shouldn't be allowed to live." They shouted, threw off their cloaks and tossed dust into the air. The captain hurried Paul into the building. They were about to whip him. Paul said, "This is against Roman law. I'm a citizen and have done no wrong."

The soldiers were afraid. They'd chained a Roman citizen and could be arrested for this. The captain didn't even know what Paul had done. So he brought the apostle to the priests and the Jewish council.

*Questions: Why were the soldiers afraid? Where did the captain take Paul?*

143

# Saved from the Jewish Council
## Acts 23:1-11

Paul addressed the council. "Brothers," he began. "I've always lived for God."

The high priest interrupted. "Hit him in the mouth!" he ordered.

"God will hit you, you whitewashed wall!" Paul came back. "You pretend to judge me by the law. But hitting me breaks the law."

"Do you dare put down God's high priest?" someone asked.

"I didn't know he was the high priest," Paul replied. "The scripture says, 'Don't speak evil of your leaders.'"

Paul explained the truth about the resurrection. "Brothers," he declared, "I'm on trial because of one thing: The hope of the resurrection of the dead." So a great hubbub began. Some wanted to let Paul go. Others refused. The argument became violent.

The Roman captain thought, "They're going to tear Paul to pieces." So the soldiers went down and took him out by force.

That night the Lord stood near Paul. "Be brave," he said. "You've spoken for me here. You'll speak for me in Rome, too."

*Questions: Why was there a hubbub in the Jewish council? Where did the Lord say Paul would speak for him?*

# Paul and 470 Soldiers
## Acts 23:12-35

The next morning more than forty people plotted against Paul. "We swear not to eat until we kill him," they agreed. They went to the council and told them their plans. "Call for Paul to come back for another meeting. We'll kill him before he gets here."

Meanwhile, Paul's nephew heard about this trap. He went to Paul and told him of the danger. "Take this young man to the captain," Paul said. "He has something important to tell him." Paul's nephew secretly told the captain about the planned ambush.

Then the captain gave these orders: "Get ready to leave by nine o'clock tonight. Take Paul to Caesarea. Call together 200 soldiers, seventy horsemen, and 200 spearmen. Provide a horse for Paul and bring him to Felix the governor." A letter was written to Felix explaining the matter. Paul's accusers were told, "Go to the governor with your problem."

That night Paul and 470 Roman soldiers left Jerusalem. At Caesarea they delivered the letter and the prisoner to the governor. "I'll hear your case. But not until your accusers get here." Paul was kept under guard in Herod's palace.

*Questions: Who saved Paul from the plotters? How many soldiers guarded Paul?*

# Paul Speaks to Felix
## Part One
### Acts 24:1-16

Five days later the high priest Ananias came down to Caesarea. Some elders and a lawyer came along. Paul entered the governor's court and the lawyer began to accuse him: "Your Excellency, thank you for the peace and favor you've given us. I'll keep this short. This man is a pest in our nation. He stirs up Jews all over the world. He's a leader of a sect called the Nazarines. He even tried to infect the temple with Gentiles. We wanted to judge him ourselves. But the captain took him away from us. That's why we're here today." Ananias joined in accusing Paul. He agreed with all the lawyer said.

Paul then spoke to Felix. "I'm happy to tell you my side of this story," he began. "I went to worship in Jerusalem twelve days ago. I didn't argue with anyone or stir up the crowds. They can't prove the things they say against me. I worship my ancestors' God, believing the law and the prophets. My hope in God is the same as their's. I do my best always to have a good heart. It is free from wrong before God and before people."

*Questions: What did Paul say about his way of worship? What did Paul say about his heart?*

# Paul Speaks to Felix
*Part Two*
*Acts 24:17-26*

Paul continued telling his story to Governor Felix:

"I came to Jerusalem bringing gifts for the poor. I simply wanted to offer sacrifices. While I did this they found me in the temple and some Jews from Asia were there. They're the ones who should be here today. They may have something against me. These men here should tell you another story. I was brought to their council. There I mentioned that God would bring us back from death. Maybe that's their problem."

Felix knew quite a bit about the Christian way. "The Roman captain must come here," he said. "Then I'll decide this matter." Guarded by soldiers, Paul had the freedom to see his friends.

A few days later Felix sent for him. The apostle explained the gospel to the governor and his wife. They heard about God's judgment. Self-control was a part of Paul's message to them. These and other things frightened Felix. "Go away for now," he told Paul. "I'll send for you again when I can." What he really wanted was payment to set Paul free. The apostle waited there for two years.

*Questions: Paul explained the gospel to Felix. What did he talk about? What did Felix want to trade for Paul's freedom?*

# Paul Dodges an Ambush
### Acts 24:27-25:12

A new governor came to power named Festus. As a favor to the Jews, he kept Paul in prison. In Jerusalem the priests and leaders gave Festus a bad report about Paul. "Do us a favor," they said. "Send Paul here. We'll settle this problem." In fact, they planned to ambush Paul and kill him.

"No," replied Festus. "I'll be in Caesarea soon. You come down, and we'll settle this." In Caesarea, the Jews falsely charged Paul, but they lacked proof.

"I've done nothing against the Jewish law," Paul replied. "I didn't pollute the temple and I always respect the Roman emperor."

Festus said, "Do you want to go to Jerusalem to settle this?"

"I've done no wrong to the Jews. You know this. I'm not trying to escape. But I've done nothing that deserves death. So no one can turn me over to them. Instead, I'll take my case to the emperor in Rome." Paul knew he'd be killed if he went back to Jerusalem.

Festus talked with his council. Then he said, "You want the emperor to hear your case. Therefore, you will go to Rome."

*Questions: Why didn't Paul want to go back to Jerusalem? Where did Paul want to take his case?*

148

# The King Hears the Gospel

## Part One
### Acts 25:13-19

Agrippa, the king of Galilee and his wife Bernice, visited Festus in Caesarea. "I'd like to hear this man Paul myself," said Agrippa. "Tomorrow," agreed Festus, "you'll hear him."

The next day King Agrippa and Bernice were escorted by military leaders and city rulers. "King Agrippa," Festus announced, "here is the man I mentioned. People claim that he should die. But he has done no wrong."

The king spoke to Paul: "You have my permission to speak."

"I'm glad to tell you my story, King Agrippa," Paul began. "You know the Jewish customs and matters of their law. Please listen patiently. I'm on trial because I believe God's promise to our ancestors. All the Jews hope for this as well. It is that God will bring us back from death. Yet now they accuse me because I believe this!

"I hated the name of Jesus. I was furious and punished Christians. I even traveled to faraway places to arrest them." Paul described what happened to him at Damascus. He told the king of his heavenly vision.

*Questions: Who was the king that heard Paul's gospel? What is God's promise that Paul mentioned to the king?*

# The King Hears the Gospel
## Part Two
### Acts 26:20-32

"'Change your mind! Turn to God!' I declared this wherever I went. I told Jews and Gentiles. That's why the Jews tried to kill me. But God has helped me. My message is the same as Moses and the prophets: Christ would suffer; he would be first to return from death; he would give light to all people."

"You're out of your mind, Paul!" exclaimed Festus.

"This is the level-headed truth," said Paul.

"Do you want me to be a Christian?" asked Agrippa.

"I want you all to be like me—except without these chains."

*Questions: What did Paul tell people wherever he went? What was Paul's gospel message?*

150

# Paul's Perilous Voyage

## Part One
### Acts 26:30-27:11

"This man has done nothing wrong," the king said as he left. "He could have been set free. But now he has to take his case to the emperor."

Paul, Luke, and Aristarchus traveled to Rome with several other prisoners. They set sail with the Roman centurion, Julius, in charge.

From Caesarea the ship sailed north along the coast of Judea. They anchored at Sidon. There Julius allowed Paul to visit his friends. The ship left the next day. It didn't land again until reaching Myra in Lycia. There the prisoners were moved to a ship from Alexandria. It was carrying wheat from Egypt to Italy.

Sailing was slow because the wind was blowing the wrong way. Finally, they came under the south side of the island of Crete. There they entered the port of Fair Havens. They had lost many days getting this far in the voyage. Winter would have to pass before they could sail on to Italy.

Paul spoke to the ship's captain and her owner: "I can see that this will be a dangerous voyage. The cargo will be lost, and so will our lives." But they paid no attention.

*Questions: Why couldn't the king set Paul free? What did Paul tell the ship's captain about the voyage?*

# Paul's Perilous Voyage
## Part Two
### Acts 27:12-26

air Havens wasn't a good place to spend the winter. "Let's take a chance and put out to sea," the captain said. "We'll try to reach Phoenix." This nearby harbor would be safe from the winter storms. They drew in the anchor and set sail close to shore. Soon a violent wind rushed down from Crete. The ship couldn't be turned to face the storm. The northeast wind drove them out to sea. Struggling for control, the crew lowered the sea anchor. The only sight was sea and sky. They were driven into the unknown.

*Questions: Why did the captain want to sail to Phoenix? What happened when the storm blew down from Crete?*

# Paul's Perilous Voyage

*Part Three*

*Acts 27:27-32*

The storm pounded violently. Soon the ship's tools, equipment, and cargo were tossed overboard. While the tempest raged, no one saw the sun or stars. All hope was lost.

Paul spoke to everyone: "Last night an angel from my God stood by me. He said, 'Don't be afraid, Paul. You must speak to the emperor in Rome. God has granted safety to those who are sailing with you.' So keep up your courage. I have faith in God. It will be just as I've been told."

Fourteen days and nights the ship drifted across the Adriatic Sea. Then, at about midnight, the sailors guessed that they were near land. Testing the water's depth they saw it was getting shallow. "We'll run onto the rocks!" they cried. Four anchors were dropped from the stern of the ship. They prayed for daylight.

In the darkness the sailors tried to leave the doomed ship. Paul told Julius the centurion, "These men must stay in the ship. If not, no one will be saved." The soldiers made sure the sailors stayed.

*Questions: What did the angel tell Paul about the men on the ship? Why did Paul say the men should keep up their courage?*

# Shipwrecked on Malta
## Acts 27:39-44

It was just before dawn on the storm-tossed ship. "We've not eaten for two weeks," said Paul. "Please, have some food. It will help you to survive." Everyone watched Paul. He took bread, gave thanks to God, broke it, and began to eat. Then all 276 people in the ship took food. Everyone ate and was satisfied. Then they threw the wheat into the sea. This made the ship float higher in the water.

When daylight broke, they could see land. There was a bay with a beach. "Run the ship aground at that beach," ordered the captain. Anchors were cast off into the sea. Steering oars were untied, ready to use. The foresail was raised and they made for the beach. But before the ship hit the sand, it struck an underwater reef. The vessel was stuck. Its stern, pounded by waves, broke up. Danger was all around.

The soldiers said, "Let's kill the prisoners or they'll escape." But Julius wanted to save Paul and wouldn't allow this.

"If you can swim, jump overboard!" ordered the captain. The others came ashore floating on pieces of the ship. Everyone was brought safely to land.

*Questions: What did Paul do before he ate? Why wouldn't Julius let the soldiers kill the prisoners?*

# Paul Arrives in Rome
### Acts 28:1-23

Paul's ship wrecked on a little island named Malta. The kind natives built a fire for the cold, wet survivors. Paul brought some brushwood to the fire. Suddenly, a snake in the brushwood bit Paul. But he shook it off into the fire. They expected Paul to drop dead. Nothing happened. The superstitious natives thought this meant Paul was a god.

The father of a Maltese nobleman named Publius lay sick. Paul put his hands on the man and prayed. He was cured. All the people on the island then brought their sick to Paul. They also were cured.

Three months later, they set sail on a ship called The Twin Brothers. Sailing in front of a south wind, the apostle finally landed in Italy. Believers from Rome walked fifty miles down the Italian coast to greet Paul. He gratefully thanked God for them.

In Rome Paul lived in his own house with a guard. The Jewish leaders visited Paul. "We've heard bad things about the Christians," they said. "But we'd like to know what you have to say." They set a day to meet with him.

*Questions: What did Paul do when he met the believers from Rome? What did the Jewish leaders in Rome want from Paul?*

155

# Salvation is Sent to the Gentiles
### Acts 28:23-28

Many Jewish leaders from Rome listened to Paul, morning to evening. By the day's end, they were arguing among themselves.

"The Holy Spirit was right," Paul said. "He said this to your ancestors: 'They'll listen, but won't catch my meaning. They'll see, but won't understand. Your words will do them no good. They won't use their eyes to look. They won't use their ears to hear. They won't understand with their minds, turn to me and be healed.'

"So I want you to know this: God's salvation has been sent to the Gentiles. They'll listen."

*Questions: What did the Jewish leaders do after they heard Paul? What did Paul say about God's salvation?*

156

# The Death of the Apostle Paul
*Acts 28:30; 2 Timothy 4:6-8*

Paul's accusers never came from Jerusalem to blame him in Rome, although he waited two years. He may have been in Spain when the city of Rome burned. It is sure that he continued traveling. Paul always cared lovingly for all the churches.

Paul visited Crete and left Titus there to help the believers. Then he went on to Miletus where his friend Trophimus got sick. Paul also visited Timothy in Ephesus. On the way he left his cloak and books in Troas. But soon he was arrested again.

Christians had been blamed for burning Rome. This may be why Paul was arrested the second time. God decided he would not be released. Instead, the apostle was convicted and beheaded by the Romans.

Before he died, Paul wrote to Timothy from prison: "It's now time for me to leave this life. I've fought a good fight. I've finished the race. I've kept the faith. The Lord has a crown waiting for me. He'll give it to me on the day he returns. Everyone who loves him and his return will get such a crown."

*Questions: How did Paul feel about all the churches? What does the Lord have waiting for people who love him?*

# John's Vision of Jesus Christ
### Part One
### *Revelation 1:9-13*

"I was in spirit on the Lord's day." These words were written by the apostle John. He was a very old man. John continued, "Behind me, I heard a loud voice like a trumpet." John was in prison because he spoke God's word. His prison was on a lonely island called Patmos. He was the last of the disciples who had walked with Jesus.

"I turned to look when I heard the voice," John wrote. "There, walking among seven gold lampstands, was Jesus Christ." John had last seen Jesus sixty years before when Jesus came back from death.

*Questions: What did Jesus's voice sound like? Where was Jesus walking when John saw him?*

158

# John's Vision of Jesus Christ
## Part Two
### Revelation 1:13-20

John saw Jesus Christ walking among the lampstands. Christ was wearing a long robe with a golden sash across his chest. His hair was as white as snow. His eyes were like flaming fire. His feet shone like polished brass in a furnace. His voice was like the sound of many rushing streams of water.

John saw seven stars in Christ's right hand. Out of his mouth came a sharp sword. His face was like the sun shining with full force. "I fell at his feet," John said, "like I was dead. But his hand touched me. 'Don't be afraid,' Christ said. 'I'm the first and the last. I'm the living one. I was dead, and look, I am alive forever and ever.'

"Then Christ said to me, 'Write down what I'll show you. Send the book to the seven churches in Asia. These seven stars are the angels of the seven churches. These gold lampstands are the seven churches.'"

John wrote a great book called the Book of Revelation. This book includes letters to the Christian churches. It also tells of the end of time. Finally, Revelation shows us what eternity with God is like.

*Questions: What did Christ say to John when he touched him? What did Christ say about himself?*

# In Eternity with God
## Revelation 21:1-22:21

"I saw a new heaven and a new earth.", John said. "The holy city, New Jerusalem, came from heaven like a bride dressed for her husband.

"A loud voice came from God's throne. The voice said, 'God's home is with humanity. He'll dwell with them; they'll be his people. God will wipe every tear from their eyes. Death will be no more. Grief, crying, and pain will be gone. Old things are passed away. I'm making everything new.'

"New Jerusalem has God's glory. It is green like jasper, clear as crystal. The twelve gates are named for Israel's twelve tribes. Each gate is a pearl. The twelve foundations are named for the Lamb's twelve apostles. These foundations are built of precious, colorful stones.

"Its one street is pure gold, transparent as glass. Out of God's throne flows the river of water of life. The tree of life grows on the river's banks. It's leaves heal the nations.

"Then Jesus said, 'The Spirit and the bride say come. Anyone who wishes may freely drink the water of life.'"

*Questions: What do the leaves of the tree of life do? What does the Spirit and the bride invite people to do?*